Masters of Modern Architecture

JOHN PETER

Masters of Modern Architecture

BONANZA BOOKS · NEW YORK

This edition published by
Bonanza Books, a division of Crown Publishers, Inc.
by arrangement with George Braziller, Inc.

© MCMLVIII by George Braziller, Inc.

Printed in the United States of America

The true work of the architect is to organize,
integrate and glorify utility. Then and then only is he
truly master-worker.

LOUIS SULLIVAN

CONTENTS

ACKNOWLEDGMENTS

The editor wishes to gratefully acknowledge the help of the following in making this book possible: Philip Johnson, Henry-Russell Hitchcock, Douglas Haskell, Jane Jacobs, Arthur Drexler and L. L. Rado for their generous good counsel; Thomas D. Parrish, and Adolf Placzek for editorial aid; Edward Mills for design; and Ezra Stoller, Julius Shulman, Hedrich-Blessing, Peter Guerrero, Kidder Smith, Lucien Hervé and others for photography; as well as people and organizations like J. M. Richards of The Architectural Review, H. M. Ottman and Anna Wong of Architectural Forum, Anthony Cardillo and Ima Cassiera of the New York Public Library, Coman Leavenworth and Nancy Riegen of the Museum of Modern Art, Miss Grace Briggs of the Harvard University Press, and Eiji Seki of the Information Office of the Consulate General of Japan, and most especially to Bob Riley, Karen Leerburger and Rosa Packard of John Peter Associates.

Note on Photographs: Several photographs have been included in this book in the interest of documentation, though they do not meet the reproduction standards of the volume as a whole.

Introduction

This is an art book of modern architecture, the great art of our times.

From the earliest ages, architecture has been a synthesis of all man's skills. It is often said to be the sum of human creativity.

Of all the arts, architecture is the typical expression of our own era. In this age of science, it is the art that has grown with engineering. In this age of machinery, it is the art that justifies mass production. In this age of sociology, it is the art that employs the talents of many people for a uniquely social end.

Modern architecture differs dramatically from the architecture of the past. But, fundamentally, both are rooted in tradition. Even today the most ancient commentaries on classical architecture can be read with profit as timeless and universal observations about the aims and methods of architecture.

The Roman architect, Vitruvius, whose *Ten Books on Architecture* is the epitome of the building art of the ancient world, stated:

I have drawn up definite rules to enable you, by observing them, to have personal knowledge of the quality of both existing buildings and those which are yet to be constructed. . . . All must be built with due reference to convenience, durability and beauty.

Lao Tse, who lived and wrote in China in the sixth century B.C., described the concept of architecture as space:

We turn clay to make a vessel; but it is on the space where there is nothing that the utility of the vessel depends. We pierce doors and windows to make a house; but it is on these spaces where there is nothing that the utility of the house depends. Therefore just as we take advantage of what is, we should recognize the utility of what is not.

The evolution of modern architecture has not been, of course, a steady progress from past successes to present successes. Nor is it possible to claim that the wisdom of the ages has always been an unqualified aid to architecture as an art. In the Age of Reason, notably, the practices of the past, rediscovered and reworked with commendable but uncritical enthusiasm, gradually eclipsed the pressing realities of present needs and architecture declined. That invigorating curiosity of the Renaissance which, through the recovery of the ideals of ancient Greece and Rome, had added immeasurably to the richness of European life, had, in the succeeding age, relapsed into a simpler fixation upon the past. Though appreciation of the ancient models had resulted, at first, in a deeper understanding and more unified approach to architectural problems, imitation came soon to mean only the unimaginative duplication of what had been done before. Architecture, both as theory and practice, suffered.

The situation in architecture, though critical, was far from fatal, for reason, as science rather than as art, was also creating the Industrial Revolution. In a cataclysm of change, the ways in which men had lived and worked were abruptly, and for all times, altered.

Factories, bridges, docks, warehouses, in ever increasing numbers, were needed to house the swelling energies of the new industrial order.

The task of industrial design fell not to the traditional architects but to the engineers whom the new industry favored. The older school of builders confined themselves more and more to plans for public buildings and mansions for the upper classes. With undiminished skill, these men decorated their buildings with odds and ends of the past. They did not lack talent. They had simply failed to recognize the times in which they lived. The "grand style" that they so lovingly evolved consisted chiefly in tacking onto their buildings Greek and Roman motifs in wood, cast iron, or plaster. In their hands, architectural design became synonymous with ornamentation.

A few men, knowing that something had gone wrong, rejected the architectural spirit of the times and suggested alternatives. But even these solutions looked back longingly to the past and not to the future. Through his *Seven Lamps of Architecture,* John Ruskin set in motion a Gothic revival:

The whole mass of architecture, found on Greek and Roman models, which we have been in the habit of building for the last three centuries, is utterly devoid of all life, virtue, honourableness, or power of doing good. It is base, unnatural, unfruitful, unenjoyable, and impious. . . . Exactly in the degree in which Greek and Roman architecture is lifeless, unprofitable, and unchristian, in that same degree our own ancient Gothic is animated, serviceable, and faithful. . . . In examining the nature of the Gothic, we conclude that one of the chief elements of power in that, and in all good architecture, was the acceptance of uncultivated and rude energy in the workman.

Others, like William Morris, busied themselves with trying to breathe life back into the old crafts movement. But, even in the pursuit of Gothic, there was something more to be discovered than the work of honest craftsmen. Eugène Viollet-le-Duc, the ingenious restorer of ancient French chateaux, wrote in his *Dictionary of French Architecture:*

It is necessary to state at first that it is impossible to separate the form of thirteenth century architecture from the structure; every member of the architecture is the consequence of a need of the structure; as in the vegetable and animal genres, it is not accident nor an appendage which produces the structure but an organic necessity. . . . This form is not the result of a caprice any more than it is only a decorative expression. It is, if you wish, a necessity of the structure.

Viollet-le-Duc had, in short, concluded that everything had to have not only a reason but also a structural reason. This emphasis upon structural function proved one of the seminal ideas of modern architecture. Here, at once, was the secret of the distinctiveness, strength, and iconoclasm of modern architecture. No master of modern architecture has completely accepted or practiced this definition of function. Nevertheless, it was largely on this platform that architects abandoned their stenciled forms and facsimiles of the past and created a style that was uniquely new.

Such an emphasis upon structural function was inevitable in an age of science; it was perhaps as inevitably a consequence that the engineer displaced the architect. The engineer knew machinery and what machinery could do. Through the machine, building parts could be made in a factory. No longer had they to be shaped on site. The advantages were obvious. Now parts could be pretested. The chances of failure were reduced. Machine methods were also faster and so helped to offset the rising cost of labor. Iron—a factory product—became the material of the Industrial Revolution. In its refinement as steel, iron is still the characteristic material of modern architecture. Construction cables, the beams that implement the luxury of glass in modern building, and also the reinforcements for cement, are extensions of the tensile strength of steel.

It is not surprising, then, that the first major works of modern architecture were made of metal and, with the notable exception of the farseeing French architect, Henri Labrouste, were designed by engineers instead of architects. Nor is it surprising that the most spectac-

The traditional façade of the Bibliothèque Nationale built in Paris in 1858 by Henri Labrouste masks a completely cast iron framework that was far ahead of its times.

ular achievements of the new age were the great nineteenth century exhibition halls, the triumphant temples of science and industry.

All of the tendencies of the revolution in architecture were realized, with public acclaim, on May 1, 1851, when Queen Victoria officially opened, in London, the "Great Exhibition of the Works of Industry of All Nations." The exhibition was housed in a huge iron and glass structure that stretched across one-third of a mile of the area of Hyde Park. The Crystal Palace, as the exhibition hall was called, was erected in some one hundred and twenty-three standardized parts which had been designed by Joseph Paxton, a former gardener. The prefabricated cast-iron sections and glass panels had been bolted together in just six months and enclosed four times the area of St. Peter's Cathedral in Rome. Here was a new kind of world wonder, fully justifying the claim of a contemporary journalist that the Crystal Palace represented "a revolution in architecture from which a new style will date."

No less conclusive was the steel tower with which the engineer Gustave Eiffel amazed the world at the Great Exhibition of 1889 in Paris. The Eiffel Tower soon became the symbol of the cultural capital of the world. At the same exhibition, the architects Dutert and Cottancin unveiled the unprecedented engineering masterpiece, the daring *Palais des Machines,* with its tremendous arched ribs of steel that rested on a hinged joint just above floor level. This pivotal base, together with the sparkling glass of the roof and walls, gave the superb enclosure an airiness that was not achieved in another building until decades later.

This glistening exhibition hall for the Great Exhibition of 1851 in Hyde Park, London, aptly christened the "Crystal Palace," was designed of cast iron and glass by the English engineer, Joseph Paxton.

The American engineer, John Augustus Roebling's Brooklyn Bridge, built in 1869, used suspended steel cables to span a remarkable distance with unrivaled lightness and ease.

The immense Galerie des Machines, by Cottancin and Dutert also erected at the famous French 1889 Exhibition enclosed a space of unprecedented dimensions with a hinged steel framework.

OPPOSITE PAGE: The Marshall Field Store built in 1887 by Henry Hobson Richardson in Chicago, Illinois, was built of solid stone but the strong, simple handling of the material helped free a generation of American architects from traditional forms.

Built for the Paris Exhibition of 1889 by the French engineer, Gustave Eiffel, this tower was an overwhelming public demonstration of the power and beauty of a metal structure.

Meanwhile, in midwestern America, where there was less emphasis upon the European distinction between architect and engineer, architects were developing a new kind of multistoried building, the skyscraper. Marshall Field's Chicago department store, though built of stone by Henry Hobson Richardson, anticipated this new development. It was soon followed by many buildings with frames of steel, as forthright in structure as in appearance, in which large areas of glass filled the regular intervals between the stone-sheathed girders and beams.

No American architect better understood the challenge of the new architecture than Louis Henri Sullivan. His works, the Guaranty Building and the Carson, Pirie, Scott Store, provided its most celebrated examples. His writings supplied its most meaningful analysis and boldest inspiration.

In *Autobiography of an Idea,* Sullivan wrote:

I could now start on the course of practical experimentations I long had in mind, which was to make an architecture based on well-defined utilitarian needs—that all practical demands of utility should be paramount as a basis of planning and design; that no architectural dictum, or tradition, or superstition, or habit should stand in the way. . . . This meant that I would put to the test a formula I had evolved through long contemplation of living things, namely that *form follows function,* which would mean in practice that architecture might again become a living art, if this formula were adhered to.

Though Sullivan clearly wrote that function implied more than mere mechanical

In the Guaranty Building of Buffalo, New York, built in 1895, Louis Sullivan developed the strong vertical organization which was to become characteristic of the American skyscraper.

BELOW: Designed with a directness that emphasized its steel cage construction, the Carson, Pirie, Scott and Company department store built in 1904 by Louis Sullivan and Dankmar Adler is an outstanding example of "The Chicago School" of architecture.

efficiency and, with masterful decorations, demonstrated that he demanded more than sheer simplicity, nevertheless the phrase "Form Follows Function," derived from him, became the battle cry of the new architecture.

Frank Lloyd Wright, a student of Sullivan's, found in the teachings of his master the inspiration to develop an independent and original architectural philosophy and style. Though his important early houses, like the Robie House and the Avery Coonley House, were virtually unnoticed in an era that was preoccupied with yet another Classic Roman Revival, Frank Lloyd Wright was, in 1900, the only practicing modern architect in the United States.

In 1901, Wright was writing like a true revolutionary:

An artist's limitations are his best friends. The machine is here to stay. It is the forerunner of the democracy that is our dearest hope. There is no more important work before the new architect now than to use this normal tool of civilization to the best advantage instead of prostituting it as he has hitherto done in reproducing with murderous ubiquity forms born of other times and other conditions and which it can only serve to destroy.

In Europe, the promising movement known as *Art Nouveau* had degenerated into a plastic phantasmagoria of flowing lines and plantlike forms, but this failure was offset by the emergence, in 1907, of the *Deutsche Werkbund* and a new program for industrial design. Here was a modern movement working *with,* not *against,* the machine age. The appointment of Peter Behrens by one of the leading German electrical firms, the A.E.G., to design their buildings, package their products, and supervise their advertising signaled the return of architecture to the ideal of total design. The A.E.G. Turbine Factory in Berlin, which Behrens designed, was modern industrial architecture as we know it today.

In 1903, the French architect August Perret, influenced by the brilliant engineering developments in his country, used modern reinforced concrete for the first time. Notre Dame de Raincy and the docks at Casablanca, his pioneering works, reflect his concept of the architect as a "poet who thinks and speaks in terms of construction."

In the early 1920's, architecture responded to the revolutions in two of the other visual arts, painting and sculpture. The abstract designs of Piet Mondrian, for example, which emphasized bright primary colors and simple basic forms, were congruent with the new structural approach in architecture. The combination of these objectives, as in the early works of the Dutchman J. J. P. Oud and the German Walter Gropius, became prime characteristics of the modern style. As head of the Bauhaus, a "university of design" founded at Weimar, Gropius acquainted a whole generation of students with the new architecture.

At this point, the story of modern architecture becomes the story of the many men who create architecture today. Of these men, two—the American Frank Lloyd Wright and the Frenchman Le Corbusier—have communicated, with unflagging vigor, the vision of genius. They are the principal pioneers, practitioners, and philosophers of modern architecture. Their writings, their plans, and their products are the vital ground swell of the movement.

To all appearances, no two architects could be more unlike. Le Corbusier is a European—more precisely, a Mediterranean. He is an intellectual, a painter, and a sculptor, and he loves the city. Wright is a midwestern American. He is a poet who loves, and is inspired by, the country. Wright's buildings embrace the same nature that Le Corbusier's defy. Wright's buildings merge with their sites; Le Corbusier's rise on pillars above them. Wright's buildings are horizontal; those of Le Corbusier are vertical.

But closer examination reveals that it is the things these men share in common that make them the two great shapers of modern architecture. Not all of Wright's buildings are horizontal and built in the country; not all of Le Corbusier's are vertical and built in the city. Both men are remarkable draftsmen with a superb sense of space. Both men are international in their outlook, their practice, and their fame. Most importantly, both of them rejected the nostalgia of the nineteenth century and accepted the machine age.

With its curved iron and glass façade, the 1897 Maison du Peuple in Brussels, designed by the Belgian architect, Victor Horta, represented an advanced use of the materials of modern architecture.

The quiet sincerity and purity with which Hendrik Petrus Berlage used brick and iron in Amsterdam's Stock Exchange Building in 1898 had a vital influence on the new architecture which made a tenet of honest use of materials.

In 1898, a Scotsman, Charles Rennie Mackintosh designed this School of Art in Glasgow with a vigor that was later recognized as a mark of modern architecture.

BELOW: The influence of the German architect, Peter Behrens can be measured not only in works like this Berlin Turbine Factory built in 1909, but in those architects like Mies van der Rohe, Walter Gropius and Le Corbusier who once worked in his office.

The flowing façade of this Barcelona apartment house, Casa Mila, built in 1910 by the Spaniard, Antonio Gaudi is typical of his work which suggests the sculptural qualities of today's concrete structures.

BELOW: Architects Greene and Greene, influenced by both Japanese and frontier traditions, handled native woods in the forthright manner exhibited in this D. R. Gamble House built in 1909 in Pasadena, California.

The design of the Steiner House in 1910 by the Viennese architect, Adolph Loos was a severe protest against decorative ornament, a protest that was to become a mark of much early modern architecture.

BELOW: In California, architects like Irving Gill combined a Spanish adobe tradition with a modern art influence to create buildings of an unadorned design like the Walter Dodge House built in Los Angeles in 1917.

This Church of Notre Dame built in 1923 in Le Raincy near Paris is an unexcelled example of the work of the Frenchman, Auguste Perret who pioneered the use of reinforced concrete in buildings.

Wright and Le Corbusier are such original stylists, however, that they defy imitation, to say nothing of duplication. It has been left to others to develop the integrated systems of modern architecture. Of these latter, none is more impressive than the dedicated Ludwig Mies van der Rohe. He has concentrated on the problem of metal structure and carried the challenge of steel with glass to an ultimate. His words reveal the basis for his sensibility to proportion:

We call it a structural approach. We don't think about the form when we start, we think about the right way to use the materials. The aesthetics, in our case, comes later, much later. That is the refinement of it. The structure is the fundamental of it.

Mies van der Rohe has been called the artist-engineer. With equal justice, the Swiss Robert Maillart can be called the engineer-sculptor. The dedication of Maillart to the use of reinforced concrete has resulted in the characteristic shell structures that he has added to the repertory of the modern architect. He says of his work:

The engineer should then free himself from the forms dictated by the tradition of older building materials, so that in complete freedom and by conceiving the problem as a whole, it would use the material to its ultimate. Perhaps then we would arrive at a new style, as in automotive and aircraft construction, as beautiful and, in the same way, determined by the nature of the material.

The work of Maillart is today carried on by men like the Italian Pier Luigi Nervi and the Spaniard Eduardo Torroja who have discovered how well it validates their mathematical approach to architecture.

That there is now a general body of theory and practice that constitutes a Modern style which is rapidly becoming as clearly defined as the Greek style or the Gothic style is perhaps most clearly evidenced by the work of talented second-generation architects who have been educated and influenced by the great early masters of modern architecture.

Modern Scandinavian architecture, as typified in the work of such men as Alvar Aalto, Gunnar Asplund, and Arne Jacobsen, blends superb craftsmanship and sympathetic use of natural materials to realize specifically human and social values. The talent and temperament of Le Corbusier have been most strongly felt in the Latin countries of Europe and the Americas: in France, Spain, Italy, and, pre-eminently, in the experimental atmosphere of South America. Italian architects, such as Luigi Figini, Gino Pollini, and Giuseppe Terragni, and Latin Americans like Oscar Niemeyer, Lucio Costa, Affonso Reidy, Marcel and Milton Roberto, and Carlos Villanueva have made notable contributions to the art of modern architecture. In Japan, the work of Antonin Raymond, a disciple of Le Corbusier, has inspired the achievements of Sutemi Horiguchi, Junzo Sakakura, and Kenzo Tange.

Many of Europe's leading architects—Mies van der Rohe, Walter Gropius, Richard Neutra, Marcel Breuer, Eliel Saarinen and Eric Mendelsohn—found in the United States a technology and an economy uniquely suited to their ideas. The teachings and examples of these men have merged with earlier American developments and produced architects like Eero Saarinen, Philip Johnson, Albert Kahn, Pietro Belluschi, George Howe, Harwell Harris, Minoru Yamasaki, I. M. Pei, and Paul Rudolph.

It is characteristic of the art of architecture that masterpieces are often created by group effort. This does not, of course, replace individual talent. Some architects have a gift for working with and through a group to accomplish results of scope and size where the efforts of any single individual might have been insufficient to the task. Such men are Raymond Hood, Wallace Harrison, and Gordon Bunshaft. Rockefeller Center, Lever House, the University of Mexico, the Rome Railway Terminal, the High Point Flats and the London County Council schools are typical masterworks of group effort.

How well modern architecture has fulfilled its potential, or even its promises, may be a matter for debate. This much is certain: There is no longer any question of substituting an architecture from the past. Traditional buildings are no longer built. Nor can they be. It is economically impossible to duplicate the craftsmanship and the materials of the past. For the first time in centuries, architecture is living in the present. Modern architecture is a fact, like the modern airplane in a modern hangar, or the modern atomic reactor in a modern laboratory.

It is a legitimate prerogative of society to evaluate modern architecture as a practical as well as an aesthetic achievement. When Le Corbusier said, in 1927, "The house is a machine for living in," he was simplifying for the sake of his point. Yet the perennial popularity of his dictum proves that people *want* to judge architecture on the basis of sheer performance. Le Corbusier's definition implies an ideal undreamed of until our time. We have indeed come to expect from modern buildings the same degree of functional efficiency that we get from our automobiles and refrigerators.

As a matter of fact, it is remarkable how well modern architecture measures up to this test. In almost every type of building—office, factory, bridge, dam, school, hospital, stadium —modern architecture, judged solely on performance, works. Only in the private family dwelling, where human needs are scaled to modest and even obsolete handicraft building methods, does modern architecture lag behind. But even here there is change. Increasing prefabrication and new appliances are creating an irresistible demand for more relevant settings.

The real challenge to modern architecture comes, as ever, from the emotional, intellectual, and spiritual needs of man. It is in fulfilling these needs that the art of architecture chiefly consists. Architecture has now scraped itself clean of the encrustations of the past. It has advanced new purposes and new forms. It has, in the process, found that barren form is not enough. It has rediscovered the inherent beauty of materials. It has learned that architecture is more a question of sculpture than of draftsmanship and that space is the secret of design. It now knows that the space between buildings is as important as the space within them. It is beginning to acknowledge that it must design the total environment of man without violating either nature or human expectations.

No one is more keenly aware of this challenge than the masters of modern architecture. They have held through the years a remarkably perceptive view of their own objectives. Their own writings, which are quoted in the pages that follow, reveal the consistency of their theories. The ninety-five major works that are illustrated in this book also evidence that they knew what they were doing and how to do it—superbly. These are the words and works of the men who created modern architecture. Here—in less than a lifetime—is what they accomplished. Never has a great architectural epoch had a more promising beginning.

Architects on Architecture

The people who know modern architecture best are the men who have created it. Here, written in styles as various as their own architecture, are the important ideas of the great men of modern architecture. To read them with a keen sense of the time when they were written is to understand better a significant development in one of the noblest arts of man.

LOUIS HENRY SULLIVAN

Among the many early pioneers of modern architecture, none was more the "voice crying in the wilderness" than Louis Henry Sullivan. It was only in retrospect that his penetrating Kindergarten Chats, written in 1901, heralded the birth of a new architectural style.

In seeking now a reasonably solid grasp on the value of the word, organic, we should at the beginning fix in mind the values of the correlated words, organism, structure, function, growth, development, form. All of these words imply the initiating pressure of a living force and a resultant structure or mechanism whereby such invisible force is made manifest and operative. The pressure, we call Function: the resultant, Form. Hence the law of function and form discernible throughout nature.

I have already cautioned you against the fugacious nature of words, their peculiar tendency to transformation in meaning while they retain the same outward form. This is because the form of a word is not, itself, truly organic; it is arbitrary, and has very little inherent capacity for change in response to a change in significance—especially if the change be a subtle one. Beyond the mechanical changes that the grammarians call declensions, conjugations, compoundings, affixes, suffixes, etc., words, when written, can be modified or developed in significance only, or nearly so, by association with other words—when they are in rhythmical, organized motion. In speech, the word is rendered more plastic: hence the value of oratory. Statically words have little significance, as you may assure yourself by consulting any dictionary; but, when once they are treated dynamically and pictorially, their power to convey thought increases enormously; still, let it always be understood that the powers are not in the words so much as in the mind and heart of him who uses them as his instrument. The thought, the feeling, the beauty is not so much in the words as in what the words suggest, or are caused to suggest, to the mind of the reader, the hearer; and this power of suggestion, of evoking responsive imagination, is the power of the artist, the poet: he who surcharges words.

Some time ago you asked what connection there might be between words and architecture. There is this immediate and important connection—that architecture, for the past several centuries, has suffered from a growing accretion of words: it is now in fact so overgrown and stifled with words that the reality has been lost to view. Words and phrases have usurped the place of function and form. Finally phrase-making has come to be an accepted substitute for architecture-making.

Now, as we two together are seeking the sense of things, as we are searching out realities, let us pronounce now, once for all, that the architecture we seek is to be a reality in function and form and that that reality shall unfold within the progressing clarity of our view.

The architecture that we see today bespeaks lost organic quality. Like a man once strong but now decrepit, it no longer functions normally. Hence its form has become abnormal. It no longer speaks in tones of ringing eloquence as of yore—it now cries out to the attentive ear with an appalling, inarticulate cry, now muffled, now piercing, but ever the wail of disorganization, the sigh of dissolution. Its features have a pallid leer, a rictus. Its eye is lutreless, its ear is dulled, its vitals atrophied. So moves it wearily on its crutch of scholarship—groping through spectacles of words.

The architecture we seek shall be as a man active, alert, supple, strong, sane. A generative man. A man having five senses all awake; eyes that fully see, ears that are attuned to every sound; a man living in his present, knowing and feeling the vibrancy of that ever-moving moment, with heart to draw it in and mind to put it out: that incessant, the portentous birth, that fertile moment which we call Today! As a man who knows his day, who loves his day, who knows and loves the exercise of life, who rightly values strength and kindliness, whose feet are on the earth, whose brain is keyed to the ceaseless song of his kind: who sees the past with kindly eye, who sees the future in a kindling vision: as a man who wills to create: So shall our art be. For to live, wholly to live, is the manifest consummation of existence.

Louis H. Sulllivan, *Kindergarten Chats and Other Writings*, George Wittenborn, Inc., New York, 1947, pp. 48–49.

FRANK LLOYD WRIGHT

Frank Lloyd Wright, pupil of Sullivan, whose words were as dramatic as his buildings, was to waken America to a new architectural era. His now famous Hull House Lectures, delivered in 1901, stated some of the fundamental attitudes of modern architecture.

No one, I hope, has come here tonight for a sociological prescription for the cure of evils peculiar to this Machine Age. For I come to you as an Architect to say my word for the right use upon such new materials as we have, of our great substitute for tools—machines. There is no thrift in any craft until the tools are mastered; nor will there be a worthy social order in America until the elements by which America does its work are mastered by American society. Nor can there be an art worth the man or the name until these elements are grasped and truthfully idealized in whatever we as a people try to make. Although these elemental truths should be commonplace enough by now, as a people we do not understand them nor do we see the way to apply them. We are probably richer in raw materials for our use as workmen, citizens or artists than any other nation—but outside mechanical genius for mere contrivance we are not good workmen, nor, beyond adventitious or propitious respect for property, are we as good citizens as we should be, nor are we artists at all. We are one and all, consciously or unconsciously, mastered by our fascinating automatic "implements," using them as substitutes for tools. To make this assertion clear I offer you evidence I have found in the field of architecture. It is still a field in which the pulse of the age throbs beneath much shabby finery and one broad enough (God knows) to represent the errors and possibilities common to our time-serving time.

Architects in the past have embodied the spirit common to their own life and to the life of the society in which they lived in the most noble of all noble records—buildings. They wrought these valuable records with the primitive tools at their command and whatever these records have to say to us today would be utterly insignificant if not wholly illegible were tools suited to another and different conditions stupidly forced to work upon them; blindly compelled to do work to which they were not fitted, work which they could only spoil.

In this age of steel and steam the tools with which civilization's true record will be written are scientific thoughts made operative in iron and bronze and steel and in the plastic processes which characterize this age, all of which we call machines. The electric lamp is in this sense a machine. New materials in the man-machines have made the physical body of this age what it is as distinguished from former ages. They have made our era the machine age—wherein locomotive engines, engines of industry, engines of light or engines of war or steamships take the place works of art took in previous history.

Any popular avenue or suburb will show the polyglot encampment displaying, on the neatly kept little plots, a theatrical desire on the part of fairly respectable people to live in chateaux, manor houses, Venetian palaces, feudal castles, and Queen Anne cottages. Many with sufficient hardihood abide in abortions of the carpenter-architect, our very own General Grant Gothic perhaps, intended to beat all the "lovely periods" at their own game and succeeding. Look within all this typical monotony-in-variety and see there the machine-made copies of handicraft originals; in fact, unless you, the householder, are fortunate indeed, possessed of extraordinary taste and opportunity, all you possess is in some degree a machine-made example of vitiated handicraft, imitation antique furniture made antique by the machine, itself of all abominations the most abominable. Everything must be curved and carved and carved and turned. The whole mass a tortured sprawl supposed artistic. And the floor-coverings? Probably machine-weavings of oriental rug patterns—pattern and texture mechanically perfect; or worse, your walls are papers with paper-imitations of old tapestry, imitation patterns and imitation textures, stamped or printed by the machine; imitations under foot, imitations overhead and imitations all around you. You are sunk in "imitation." Your much-moulded woodwork is stained "antique." Inevitably you have a white-and-gold "reception-room" with a few gilded chairs, an overwrought piano, and withal, about you a general cheap machine-made "profusion" of—copies of copies of original imitations. To you, proud proprietors—do these things thus degraded mean anything aside from vogue and price? Aside from your sense of quantitative ownership, do you perceive in them some fine fitness in form, line and color to the purposes which they serve? Are the chairs to sit in, the tables to use, the couch comfortable, and are all harmoniously related to each other and to your life? Do many of the furnishings or any of the window-millinery serve any purpose at all of which you can think? Do you enjoy in "things" the least appreciation of truth in beautiful guise? If not, you are a victim of habit, a habit evidence enough of the stagnation of an outgrown art. Here we have the curse of stupidity—a cheap substitute for ancient art and craft which has no vital meaning in your own life or our time. You line the box you live in as a magpie lines its nest. You need not be ashamed to confess your ignorance of the meaning of all this, because not only you, but every one else, is hopelessly ignorant concerning it; it is "impossible." Imitations of imitations, copies of copies, cheap expedients, lack of integrity, some few blind gropings for simplicity to give hope to the picture. That is all.

Why wonder what has become of the grand spirit of art that made, in times past, man's reflection in his environment a godlike thing. *This* is what has become of it! Of all conditions, this one at home is most deplorable, for to the homes of this country we must look for any beginning of the awakening of an artistic conscience which will change this parasitic condition to independent growth. The homes of the people will change before public buildings can possibly change.

. . . For centuries this insensate or insane abuse of great opportunity in the name of culture has made cleanly, strengthy and true simplicity impossible in art or architecture, whereas now we might reach the heights of creative art. Rightly used the very curse machinery puts upon handicraft should emancipate the artist from temptation to petty structural deceit and end this wearisome struggle to make things seem what they are not and can never be. Then the machine itself, eventually, will satisfy the simple terms of its modern art equation as the ball of clay in the sculptor's hand yields to his desire—ending forever this nostalgic masquerade led by a stultified culture in the name of art.

Yes, although he does not know it, the artist is now free to work his rational will with freedom unknown to structural tradition. Units of construction have enlarged, rhythms have been simplified and etherealized, space is more spacious and the sense of it may enter into every building, great or small. The architect is no longer hampered by the stone arch of the Romans or by the stone beam of the Greeks. Why then does he cling to the grammatical phrases of those ancient methods of construction when such phrases are in his modern work empty lies, and himself an inevitable liar as well.

Already, as stand today, the machine has weakened the artist to the point of destruction and antiquated the craftsman altogether. Earlier forms of art are by abuse all but destroyed. The whole matter has been reduced to mere pose. Instead of joyful creation we have all around about us poisonous tastes—foolish attitudes. With some little of the flame of the old love, and creditable but pitiful mischief with lofty motives; perhaps, because his heart has not kept in touch or in sympathy with his scientific brother's head, being out of step with the forward marching of his own time.

. . . Grasp and use the power of scientific automatons in this *creative sense,* and their terrible forces are not antagonistic to any fine individualistic quality in man. He will find their collective mechanistic forces capable of bringing to the individual a more adequate life, and the outward expression of the inner man as seen in his environment will be genuine revelation of his inner life and higher purpose. Not until then will America be free!

This new American liberty is of the sort that declares man free only when he has found his work and effective means to achieve a life of his own. The means once found, he will find his due place. The man of our country will thus make his own way, and *grow* to the natural place thus due him, promised—yes, promised by our charter, the Declaration of Independence. But this place of his is not to be made over to fit him by reform, nor shall it be brought down to him by concession, but will become his by his own use of the means at hand. He must *himself* build a new world. The day of the individual is not over—instead, it is just about to begin. The machine does not write the doom of liberty, but is waiting at man's hand as a peerless tool, for him to use to put foundations beneath a genuine democracy. Then the machine may conquer human drudgery to some purpose, taking it upon itself to broaden, lengthen, strengthen and deepen the life of the simplest man. What limits do we dare imagine to an art that is organic fruit of an adequate life for the individual! Although this power is now murderous, chained to botchwork and bunglers' ambitions, the creative artist will take it surely into his hand and, in the name of liberty, swiftly undo the deadly mischief it has created.

Quotation from "The Art and Craft of the Machine" which appears in *The Future of Architecture* by Frank Lloyd Wright, published by Horizon Press, New York. The first statement on this subject in the twentieth century.

LE CORBUSIER

Le Corbusier stood where the widening stream of the new architectural style merged with modern abstract art. He became an articulate spokesman for international architecture with the publication of his book Towards a New Architecture *in 1923.*

There is a formidable industrial activity at present in progress, which is inevitably and constantly at the back of our minds; at every moment either directly, or through the medium of newspapers and reviews, we are presented with objects of an arresting novelty whose why and wherefore engrosses our minds, and fills us with delight and fear. All these objects of modern life create, in the long run, a modern state of mind. Bewilderment seizes us, then, if we bring our eyes to bear on the old and rotting buildings that form our snail-shell, our habitation, which crush us in our daily contact with them—putrid and useless and unproductive. Everywhere can be seen machines which serve to produce something and produce it admirably, in a clean sort of way. The machine that we live in is an old coach full of tuberculosis. There is no real link between our daily activities at the factory, the office or the bank, which are healthy and useful and productive, and our activities in the bosom of the family which are handicapped at every turn. The family is everywhere being killed and men's minds demoralized in servitude to anachronisms.

Every man's mind, being moulded by his participation in contemporary events, has consciously or unconsciously formed certain desires; these are inevitably connected with the family, an instinct which is the basis of society. Every man to-day realizes his need of sun, of warmth, of pure air and clean floors; he has been taught to wear a shiny white collar, and women love fine white linen. Man feels to-day that he must have intellectual diversion, relaxation for his body, and the physical culture needed to recuperate him after the tension of muscle or brain which his labour—"hard labour"—brings. This mass of desires constitutes in fact a mass of *demands*.

Now our social organization has nothing ready which can answer these needs.

Another point: what are the conclusions of the *intellectuals* face to face with the actualities of modern life?

The magnificent flowering of industry in our epoch has created a special class of intellectuals so numerous that it constitutes the really active stratum of society.

In the workshop, in the technical departments, in the learned Societies, in the banks and in the great stores, on newspapers and reviews, there are the engineers, the heads of departments, legal representatives, secretaries, editors, accountants who work out minutely, in accordance with their duty, the formidable things which occupy our attention: there are the men who design our bridges, ships and airplanes, who create our motors and turbines, who direct the workshops and yards, who are engaged in the distribution of capital and in accountancy, who do the purchasing of goods in the colonies or from the factory, who put forth so many articles in the Press on the modern production of so much that is noble and horrible, who record as on a chart the high-temperature curve of a humanity in labour, in perpetual labour, at a crisis—sometimes in delirium. All human material passes through their hands. In the end their observation must lead them to some conclusion. These people have their eyes fixed on the display of goods in the great shops that man has made for himself. The modern age is spread before them, sparkling and radiant . . . on the far side of the barrier! In their own homes, where they live in a precarious ease, since their remuneration bears no real relation to the quality of their work, they find their uncleanly old snail-shell, and they cannot even think of having a family. If they do so there will begin the slow martyrdom that we all know. These people, too, claim their rights to a machine for living in, which shall be in all simplicity a *human* thing.

Both the worker and the intellectual are precluded from following their deepest instincts in regard to the family; each and every day they make use of the brilliant and effective tools that the age has provided, but they are not enabled thereby to use them for themselves. Nothing could be more discouraging or more irritating. Nothing is prepared. We may well say: Architecture or Revolution.

. . . The advent of a new period only occurs after long and quiet preparatory work.

Industry has created its tools.

Business has modified its habits and customs.

Construction has found new means.

Architecture finds itself confronted with new laws.

Industry has created new tools . . . such tools are capable of adding to human welfare and of lightening human toil. If these new conditions are set against the past, you have Revolution.

Business has modified its customs: it bears a heavy responsibility to-day: cost, time, solidity of the work. Engineers in numbers fill its offices, make their calculations, practise the laws of economy to an intensive degree, and seek to harmonize two opposed factors: cheapness and good work. Intelligence lies behind every initiative, bold innovations are demanded. The morality of industry has been transformed: big business is to-day a healthy and moral organism. If we set this new fact against the past, we have Revolution in method and in the scale of the adventure.

Construction has discovered its methods, methods which in themselves mean a liberation that earlier ages had sought in vain. Everything is possible by calculation and invention, provided that there is at our disposal a sufficiently perfected body of tools, and this does exist. Concrete and steel have entirely transformed the constructional organisation hitherto known, and the exactitude with which these materials can be adapted to calculation and theory every day provides encouraging results, both in the success achieved and in their appearance, which recalls natural phenomena and constantly reproduces experiences realized in nature. If we set ourselves against the past, we can then appreciate the fact that new formulas have been found which only need exploitation to bring about (if we are wise enough to break with routine) a genuine liberation from the constraints we have till now been subjected to. There has been Revolution in methods of construction.

Architecture finds itself confronted with new laws. Construction has undergone innovations so great that the old "styles," which still obsess us, can no longer clothe it; the materials employed evade the attentions of the decorative artist. There is so much novelty in the forms and rhythms furnished by these constructional methods, such novelty in arrangement and in the new industrial programmes, that we can no longer close our minds to the true and profound laws of architecture which are established on mass, rhythm and proportion: the "styles" no longer exist, they are outside our ken; if they still trouble us, it is as parasites. If we set ourselves against the past, we are forced to the conclusion that the old architectural code, with its mass of rules and regulations evolved during four thousand years, is no longer of any interest; it no longer concerns us: all the values have been revised; there has been revolution in the conception of what Architecture is.

Disturbed by the reactions which play upon him from every quarter, the man of to-day is conscious, on the one hand, of a new world which is forming itself regularly, logically and clearly, which produces in a straightforward way things which are useful and usable, and on the other hand he finds himself, to his surprise, living in an old and hostile environment. This framework is his lodging; his town, his street, his house or his flat rise up against him useless, hinder him from following in his leisure the organic development of his existence, which is to create a family and to live, like every animal on this earth and like all men of all ages, an organized family life. In this way society is helping forward the destruction of the family, while she sees with terror that this will be her ruin.

There reigns a great disagreement between the modern state of mind, which is an admonition to us, and the stifling accumulation of age-long detritus.

The problem is one of adaptation, in which the realities of our life are in question.

Society is filled with a violent desire for something which it may obtain or may not. Everything lies in that: everything depends on the effort made and the attention paid to these alarming symptoms.

Architecture or Revolution.

Revolution can be avoided.

From Le Corbusier, *Towards a New Architecture* (translated from the French by Frederick Etchells), London, The Architectural Press, 1952.

WALTER GROPIUS

Walter Gropius, the architect-educator, early recognized the implication of mass production. In writing like this recent extract from "Scope of Total Architecture," published in 1943, he urged group practice and group planning to meet changing architectural conditions.

I should like to attempt to outline the potential strategic aim of planning for my own profession, architecture, within the cultural and political context of our industrial civilization. I shall try first to give a definition: Good planning I conceive to be both a science and an art. As a science, it analyzes human relationships; as an art, it co-ordinates human activities into a cultural synthesis. I want to put the emphasis particularly on the art of planning. Here, I believe, lie waiting creative potentialities that would give meaning and direction to our countless, isolated efforts.

We talk so much about the fact that the rapid development of science has cut so sharply into the familiar pattern of our existence that we are left with nothing but loose ends. In his eternal curiosity man learned to dissect his world with the scalpel of the scientist, and in the process has lost his balance and his sense of unity. Our scientific age, by going to extremes of specialization, has obviously prevented us from seeing our complicated life as an entity. The average professional man, driven to distraction by the multiplicity of problems spread out before him, seeks relief from the pressure of general responsibilities by picking out one single, rigidly circumscribed responsibility in a specialized field and refuses to be answerable for anything that may happen outside this field. A general dissolution of context has set in and naturally resulted in shrinking and fragmentating life. As Albert Einstein once put it: "Perfection of means and confusion of aims seem to be characteristic of our age."

Our society has certainly recognized the essential value of the scientist for its survival. We are very little aware, however, of the vital importance of the creative artist when it comes to controlling and shaping our environment. In contrast to the process of mechanization, the work of the true artist consists of an unprejudiced search for expression that symbolizes the common phenomena of life. This requires that he take an independent, uninhibited view of the whole life process. His work is most essential for the development of a true democracy, for he is the prototype of "whole" man; his freedom and independence are relatively intact. His intuitive qualities should be the antidote against over-mechanization, apt to rebalance our life and to humanize the impact of the machine. Unfortunately the artist has become the forgotten man, almost ridiculed and thought of as a superfluous luxury member of society. My belief is that, on the contrary, our disoriented society badly needs participation in the arts as an essential counterpart of science in order to stop its atomistic effect on us.

Examining our own experiences, we know that it is only in isolated cases that sober scientific facts can, all by themselves, stir the imagination to a point where people become willing to subordinate cherished personal ambitions to a common cause. Much deeper chords must be struck than those reached by analytical information if we want to call forth an enthusiastic, contagious response, capable of sweeping away barriers that stand now in the way of better planning and housing. Though scientific progress has reached us in the form of materialistic abundance and physical well-being, it has rarely matured into producing form. Consequently we find that our emotional demands remain unsatisfied by the mere material production of the eight-hour working day. This failure to gladden the soul must be the reason why we have not always been able to make our brilliant scientific and technical achievements count, and why a cultural pattern that should have emerged has, so far, eluded us.

I am convinced, therefore, that the contribution of the creative designer whose art can realize more fully the visual aspects and the human appeal of planning is essential. No society of the past has produced cultural expression without the participation of the artist; social problems cannot be solved through intellectual processes or political action only.

I speak of the great necessity to recover through every man's education the lost quality of understanding and creating form.

Think of those essential imponderables, apparent in cities and towns of bygone cultures, which still have the power to move us emotionally today, though they are obsolete from the point of view of practical use. These imponderables characterize what is missing in the concept of our present communities, namely, that unity of order and spirit which is forever significant, visibly expressed in space and volume.

Planners experience in their daily work that the public is still very ignorant of the great benefits awaiting it from good planning. The average citizen is inclined to see an interference with the personal freedom when given direction by government agencies. The necessity continuously to inform him why communal planning is to his own best advantage calls for the highest psychological ability in a planner. A systematic psychological training in "basic politics" should give the planning student the understanding of cause and effect of human behavior. It should teach him how to put into his own practice persuasion, tact, patience, and appreciation of the thought and position of others as the most effective tools of planning.

Today we still meet too often with a deep-rooted inclination to dodge a large-scale conception for planning and housing and to add up, instead, unrelated piecemeal improvements. This will change only with a growing community spirit, carefully nurtured on all educational levels until it becomes a subconscious attitude of everybody and may finally cause a chain reaction conducive to solving our collective task.

Such an educational framework, as here indicated, also seems to have qualities favorable for the advancement of genuine teamwork which will naturally develop more and more in the future with the ever widening horizon of our physical knowledge of which each of us commands only a small segment. The task is too big for individuals alone. After almost twenty-five years of most valuable research and formulation of our ideas, we seem now to be in urgent need of action in groups. For in spite of the wealth of theoretical thought on community living which has been accumulated in recent years, hardly any new comprehensive "experiments in living" have been made. There is no other way toward progress but to start courageously and without prejudice new practical tests by building model communities in one stroke and then systematically examining their living value. What a wealth of new information for the sociologist, the economist, the scientist and the artist would be forthcoming, if groups, formed of the most able planners and architects available, should be commissioned to design and build completely new model communities: Such information would also offer most valuable preparatory data to solve the complicated problem of rehabilitating our existing communities. The blocks which have to be removed before we can create such laboratories for living are obviously political and legal in character. Without duly accepted legal instruments, one community master plan after the other will become a symbol of wishful thinking, of agonizing frustration.

I have come to the conclusion that an architect or planner worth the name must have a very broad and comprehensive vision indeed to achieve a true synthesis of a future community. This we might call "total architecture." To do such a total job he needs the ardent passion of a lover and the humble willingness to collaborate with others, for great as he may be he cannot do it alone. The kinship of regional architectural expression which we so much desire will greatly depend, I believe, on the creative development of teamwork. Abandoning the morbid hunt for "styles" we have already started to develop together certain attitudes and principles which reflect the new way of life of twentieth-century man. We have begun to understand that designing our physical environment does not mean to apply a fixed set of esthetics, but embodies rather a continuous inner growth, a conviction which recreates truth continually in the service of mankind.

From Walter Gropius, *Scope of Total Architecture*, New York, Harper & Brothers, 1943, pp. 171, 175–176, 178–179, 185.

LUDWIG MIES VAN DER ROHE

Ludwig Mies van der Rohe is dedicated to structural perfection in an age of science. In this talk, given in 1953 on the occasion of his appointment as head of the Department of Architecture at Armour Institute, he defined the relationship of architecture and technology.

Technology is rooted in the past. It dominates the present and tends into the future. It is a real historical movement—one of the great movements which shape and represent their epoch. It can be compared only with the Classic discovery of man as a person, the Roman will to power, and the religious movement of the Middle Ages. Technology is far more than a method, it is a world in itself. As a method it is superior in almost every respect. But only where it is left to itself as in gigantic structures of engineering, there technology reveals its true nature. There it is evident that it is not only a useful means, that it is something, something in itself, something that has a meaning and a powerful form—so powerful in fact, that it is not easy to name it. Is that still technology or is it architecture? And that may be the reason why some people are convinced that architecture will be outmoded and replaced by technology. Such a conviction is not based on clear thinking. The opposite happens. Wherever technology reaches its real fulfillment, it transcends into architecture. It is true that architecture depends on facts, but its real field of activity is in the realm of significance. I hope you will understand that architecture has nothing to do with the invention of forms. It is not a playground for children, young or old. Architecture wrote the history of the epochs and gave them their names. Architecture depends on its time. It is the crystallization of its inner structure, the slow unfolding of its form. That is the reason why technology and architecture are so closely related. Our real hope is that they grow together, that someday the one be the expression of the other. Only then will we have an architecture worthy of its name: Architecture as a true symbol of our time.

From Philip C. Johnson, *Mies van der Rohe,* New York, Museum of Modern Art, 1953, pp. 203, 204.

PIER LUIGI NERVI

Of the men who have introduced new shapes to modern architecture, none has been more practical and imaginative than the engineer Pier Luigi Nervi. Taken from a talk given during his recent tour of the United States, this excerpt states his faith in the beauty of structure.

During the last one hundred years all the factors which directly or indirectly influenced construction have been harmoniously directed towards a new architecture which has no real connection with the past.

Nothing is more absurd or sterile than to try to maintain, artificially, structural schemes and architectural forms of a past which have nothing in common with the present or with the foreseeable future.

On the basis of these considerations, it may be well to ask ourselves what will be the direction of this new architecture.

It is easy to observe that the increasing importance of the structural aspects of the new themes (like long-span bridges, great halls, stadiums, railroads, maritime and air terminals, large factories and large office and storage buildings) require a strict adherence to what I like to call "statical truth" in order to obtain economical and constructionally possible solutions.

It is obvious that any structure of large dimensions is strictly limited by structural requirements, both in its form and in its resisting skeleton.

The freedom to select structural forms, such as the head of a window or the arch of a cloister—the structural elements of the architecture of the past—no longer exists when we are confronted with large dimensions or exceptionally heavy loads. A bridge more than 100 ft in span has already a limited number of solutions; if the span is over 150 ft, the number of possible solutions decreases; and there may be only one or two solutions left when the span is over 300 ft. The profile of an arch-bridge of more than 300 or 400 ft span cannot differ much from the curve of the resultant pressures of the permanent load. Therefore its shape will be very near the shape of a parabola.

Every important piece of construction will therefore have a tendency to express, more and more, the structural scheme which determines it. Actually an honest expression of such a scheme will be architecturally eloquent.

Numerous realizations in other technical fields help us in the creation of a new esthetic sentiment which necessarily is deeply felt in architecture. Airplanes, ships, automobiles and machines cannot help obeying the strictest functional truths and the rigorous laws of statics and dynamics which leave us little room for fantastic creations.

In the eighteenth century a complete freedom of form and of decorative detail allowed the builder of sailing ships and of horse-drawn carriages the creation of beautiful looking vessels and magnificent berlines. These products were in complete esthetic accord with the architecture, the interior decoration and the fashions of the time.

The shapes of our airplanes, our ships and our automobiles are rapidly approaching standard shapes of minimum resistance. In a few years they will have to adhere to theoretical aerodynamic hydrodynamic shapes, whatever the esthetic feelings of their builders.

It is therefore foreseeable that both because of the direct influence of the structural problems of large structures and because of the direct influence of other technical and mechanical realizations, and finally because of the ever-increasing influence of economic factors, the entire architecture of the future will be directed towards truth; that is, towards a more truthful style.

This new direction which tomorrow's architecture must inevitably take (unless all the fundamental technical aspects of our new culture should suddenly be revolutionized) will not lead us necessarily to cold and standard architectural expressions. First of all, the structural forms of great works are in themselves rich and beautiful; but, moreover, we must create architectural expressions of minor importance which are at the same time functionally and economically correct, free of useless and often vulgar decorations, made interesting by harmonious relations of volumes and surfaces and enriched by color and by the refinement of details.

Then there are entire fields of architecture which always will be free from the cold and purely technical requirements of structuralism. For example, the solution of urban problems in the residential sections of our cities can still be quite free and may express in the serene joy of their green areas the need for romanticism and poetry which, I hope, will still be felt by future generations.

After so many changes due to the varying sensibilities and to the social conditions of humanity in the past, we now see the birth of this new "style of truth" which is imposed by the techniques of mechanics and of large structures and which will invade all other fields of human activity.

All over the world, new structures are being built today which more or less consciously express this style of truth. I believe that in the near future this style will flourish consciously everywhere.

From Pier Luigi Nervi, "The Place of Structure in Architecture," *Architectural Record,* July, 1956, pp. 189–191.

RICHARD NEUTRA

Richard Neutra reemphasizes the application of modern biological and sociological sciences to architecture in this excerpt from his recent book "Life and Human Habitat."

The duality of a separate beauty and utility surely does not exist in outer nature around us, which, after all, is our precedent. When does a parrot or a blooming tree stop being beautiful and start to be utilitarian? Any answer here would be silly.

But this same, troublesome, fuzzy-brained duality also has no real base in our natural "body-soul make-up." Certainly among all the millions of sense receptors known to science as continuously active in a human being, no separate "sense of beauty" has ever been discovered.

It is simply an old figure of speech, but far from harmless. Confused by it, we always seem engaged in a losing battle with that "other sense for practical reality." Deep satisfaction depends on a miraculously harmonized reception, that comprises and fuses everything.

The falsehood of that other approach keeps on producing a cleavage, a pernicious split in the man-made environment of our day. It is this falsehood and confusion of attitude which can be blamed for the barbarism, litter and jam of our civilization so famous for its "know-how" and so offensive to our nerves. Why can we not organize the shapes around us, even in our most prosperous American cities?

Can we stand a painfully chopped-up setting or is our very nature frustrated by it? The human organic system is an entity, a oneness. There are fluid nervous connections, uninterrupted. Nothing is truly departmentalized in man. The intellect, the emotions, the "impure" and the "pure" reason are only old-fashioned labels, confounding the picture of our perpetually inter-twined vital flow of life processes—nervous, glandular, muscular. When this harmony is broken, harm begins, and, perceptibly or not, leads to withering, stoppage and death. It is these life processes which we architects ourselves can help or harm. It is these life processes which we must elastically house and accommodate, if we want to be responsible designers of this so powerful, influential, constructed and fabricated environment, of buildings, neighborhoods, towns. No material is as interesting to us as the human. Tremendous research on the strains and stresses which we can produce in this responsive, subtle material is already very much on hand, and done by biologists and physiologists. Their enlightening continues and spreads from year to year. We architects of tomorrow must be as curious as were those scientifically minded artists of the Renaissance, and we are, at least, not as lonesome, illicit and solitary with our curiosity as was Leonardo da Vinci.

If man, woman and child alive are our subject of love and study, we must recognize that they are not governed by some over-simplified, static, geometrical, or mystic "modulor."

Much diversified and carefully graded experimentation will be necessary to give ever greater clarity to means and purposes of the architect, which all deal with applied human biology. Man remains the measure and the center of his world.

This broad, systematic progress is yet in the future, but the client of a domestic project sits with his wife, very visibly and audibly before us. We can learn in practice how to conduct a revealing clinical interrogation—and learn the decisive earnestness of it all for any other broader, more voluminous projects to come.

"Architecture of architects" has *often* been way below the instinctive level of biological understanding and in-feeling which is frequently found in folklore architecture. Architecture and urban design as a profession may and will reach and, we may hope, surpass these more innocent levels, only with the help of our current stupendous progress in the life sciences, which permit us designers to "know man" better than he has ever been known. We must only wish and work for it, and a grand future for this vital development spreads before us wondrously. It is infinite, and wholesome, not fashion-ridden, and hectically "quick turnover." This is the bright outlook for the young man to be steadily engaged in architecture, as an ever more subtle and suitable environmental design for the happier survival of mankind.

From Richard J. Neutra, *Life and Human Habitat*, George Wittenborn Inc., New York.

FRANK LLOYD WRIGHT   UNITY TEMPLE   OAK PARK, ILLINOIS, 1906

FRANK LLOYD WRIGHT   AVERY COONLEY HOUSE   RIVERSIDE, ILLINOIS, 1908

FRANK LLOYD WRIGHT

FREDERICK C. ROBIE HOUSE
CHICAGO, ILLINOIS, 1909

44

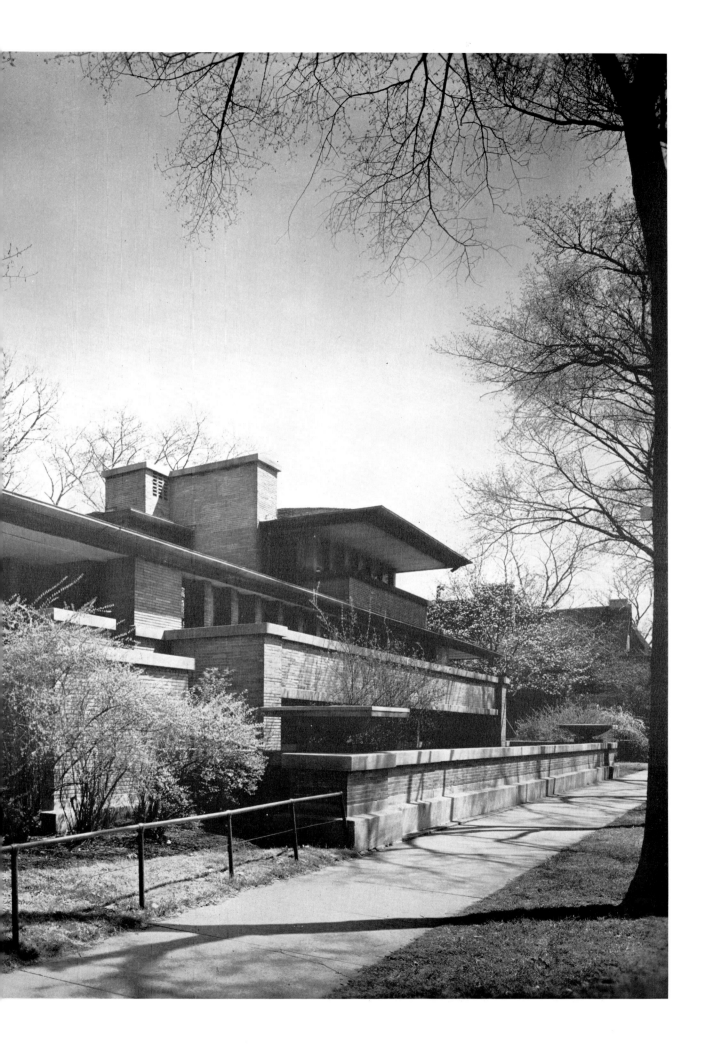

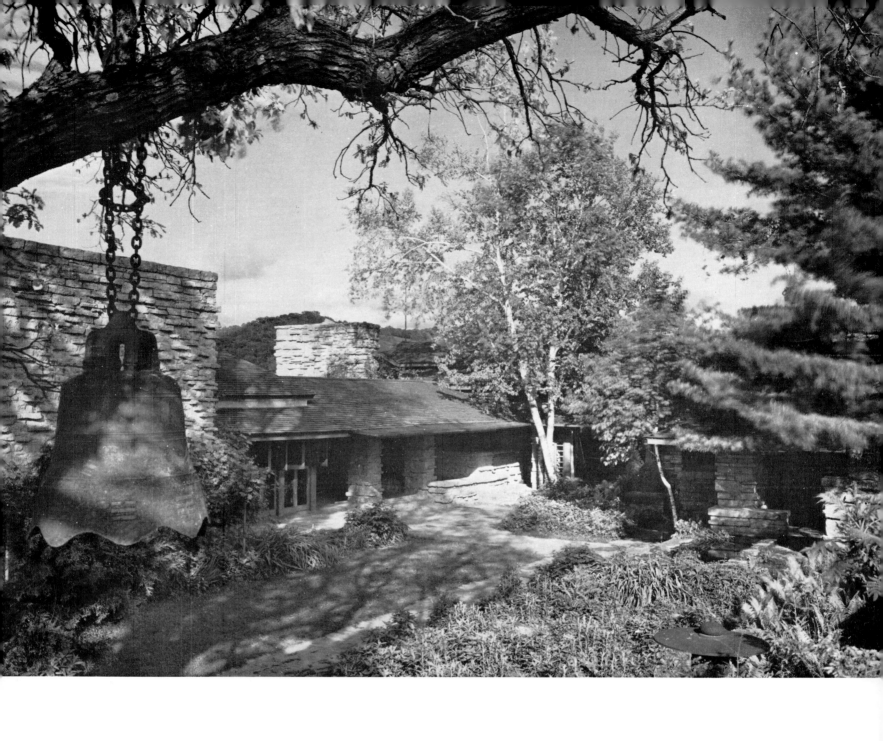

FRANK LLOYD WRIGHT   TALIESIN   SPRING GREEN, WISCONSIN, 1914

FRANK LLOYD WRIGHT   GEORGE MADISON MILLARD HOUSE   PASADENA, CALIFORNIA, 1923

FRANK LLOYD WRIGHT   CHARLES ENNIS HOUSE   LOS ANGELES, CALIFORNIA, 1924

FRANK LLOYD WRIGHT

"FALLING WATER," EDGAR J. KAUFMANN HOUSE
BEAR RUN, PENNSYLVANIA, 1936

FRANK LLOYD WRIGHT

S. C. JOHNSON & SON, INC., BUILDINGS
RACINE, WISCONSIN, 1936–1939

53

FRANK LLOYD WRIGHT   TALIESIN WEST   PARADISE VALLEY, NEAR PHOENIX, ARIZONA, 1938–

FRANK LLOYD WRIGHT   ROSE PAUSON HOUSE   PHOENIX, ARIZONA, 1940

FRANK LLOYD WRIGHT   H. C. PRICE TOWER   BARTLESVILLE, OKLAHOMA, 1953–1956

LE CORBUSIER   SINGLE HOUSE FOR THE STUTTGART EXHIBITION   STUTTGART, GERMANY, 1927

LE CORBUSIER AND PIERRE JEANNERET

SAVOYE HOUSE
POISSY-SUR-SEINE, FRANCE, 1928–1930

64

LE CORBUSIER

UNITE D'HABITATION
MARSEILLES, FRANCE, 1943–1950

LE CORBUSIER   CHAPEL OF NOTRE DAME-DU-HAUT   RONCHAMP, FRANCE, 1950–1955

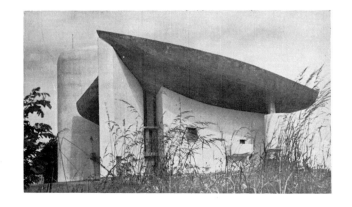

LE CORBUSIER, WITH PIERRE JEANNERET,
E. MAXWELL FRY AND JANE DREW

HIGH COURT BUILDING
CHANDIGARH, INDIA, 1957-

LUDWIG MIES VAN DER ROHE

GERMAN PAVILION AT THE INTERNATIONAL EXPOSITION
BARCELONA, SPAIN, 1929

LUDWIG MIES VAN DER ROHE   TUGENDHAT HOUSE   BRNO, CZECHOSLOVAKIA, 1930

LUDWIG MIES VAN DER ROHE

CAMPUS, ILLINOIS INSTITUTE OF TECHNOLOGY
CHICAGO, ILLINOIS, 1939–

LUDWIG MIES VAN DER ROHE   EDITH FARNSWORTH HOUSE   PLANO, ILLINOIS, 1950

LUDWIG MIES VAN DER ROHE

860 LAKE SHORE DRIVE APARTMENT HOUSES
CHICAGO, ILLINOIS, 1951

LUDWIG MIES VAN DER ROHE AND PHILIP JOHNSON
SEAGRAM BUILDING
NEW YORK, NEW YORK, 1958

WALTER GROPIUS   FAGUS WORKS   ALFELD, GERMANY, 1911

WALTER GROPIUS   BAUHAUS   DESSAU, GERMANY, 1926

WALTER GROPIUS   MUNICIPAL EMPLOYMENT OFFICE   DESSAU, GERMANY, 1928

RICHARD J. NEUTRA   LOVELL HOUSE   LOS ANGELES, CALIFORNIA, 1929

ROBERT MAILLART   SALGINATOBEL BRIDGE   SWITZERLAND, 1929–1930

ROBERT MAILLART   SCHWANDBACH BRIDGE   BERNE, SWITZERLAND, 1933

ROBERT MAILLART
BRIDGE OVER THE RIVER THUR
NEAR SAINT-GALLI, SWITZERLAND, 1933

MARCEL BREUER AND ALFRED AND EMIL ROTH
DOLDERTHAL APARTMENTS
ZURICH, SWITZERLAND, 1934

RICHARD J. NEUTRA   EXPERIMENTAL SCHOOL   LOS ANGELES, CALIFORNIA, 1934–1935

EDUARDO TORROJA   HIPPODROME   MADRID, SPAIN, 1935

ROBERT MAILLART   BRIDGE OVER RIVER ARVE   SWITZERLAND, 1936–1937

LUCIO COSTA, OSCAR NIEMEYER, AFFONSO REIDY,
CARLOS LEAO, JORGE MOREIRA
AND HERNANI VASCONCELOS;
LE CORBUSIER, CONSULTANT

MINISTRY OF EDUCATION AND HEALTH
RIO DE JANEIRO, BRAZIL, 1937–1943

ALVAR AALTO   SUNILA FACTORY, HOUSES AND PULP MILLS   FINLAND, 1937–1939

ELIEL AND EERO SAARINEN

TABERNACLE CHURCH OF CHRIST
COLUMBUS, INDIANA, 1942

111

PIER LUIGI NERVI   MILITARY HANGARS   ORBITELLO, ITALY, 1938–1942

114

WALTER GROPIUS AND MARCEL BREUER   CHAMBERLAIN HOUSE   SUDBURY, MASSACHUSETTS, 1939

OSCAR NIEMEYER

CHURCH OF ST. FRANCIS OF ASSISI
PAMPULHA, BRAZIL, 1943

RICHARD J. NEUTRA
CHANNEL HEIGHTS HOUSING PROJECT
SAN PEDRO, CALIFORNIA, 1943–1944

MARCEL BREUER   ROBINSON HOUSE   WILLIAMSTOWN, MASSACHUSETTS, 1946

PIER LUIGI NERVI   SALT WAREHOUSE   TORTONA, ITALY, 1950

THE ARCHITECTS' COLLABORATIVE

HARVARD UNIVERSITY GRADUATE CENTER
CAMBRIDGE, MASSACHUSETTS, 1949–1950

EERO SAARINEN   GENERAL MOTORS TECHNICAL CENTER   DETROIT, MICHIGAN, 1951–1957

128

OSCAR NIEMEYER

OSCAR NIEMEYER HOUSE
RIO DE JANEIRO, BRAZIL, 1953–1954

EERO SAARINEN

MASSACHUSETTS INSTITUTE OF TECHNOLOGY,
KRESGE AUDITORIUM AND CHAPEL
CAMBRIDGE, MASSACHUSETTS, 1955

EDUARDO TORROJA WITH M. BARBERO AND G. ECHEGARAY
TECHNICAL INSTITUTE OF CONCRETE CONSTRUCTION   MADRID, SPAIN, 1955

PIER LUIGI NERVI (ENGINEER), ANNIBALE VITELLOZZI (ARCHITECT)
OLYMPIC SPORTS PALACE   ROME, ITALY, 1957

J. J. P. OUD   WORKER'S HOUSES   HOOK OF HOLLAND, HOLLAND, 1926–1927

BRINKMAN & VAN DER VLUGT

VAN NELLE TOBACCO, TEA AND COFFEE FACTORY
ROTTERDAM, HOLLAND, 1928–1930

138

ERIC MENDELSOHN

SCHOCKEN DEPARTMENT STORE
CHEMNITZ, GERMANY, 1928–1930

WILLEM DUDOK

TOWN HALL
HILVERSUM, HOLLAND, 1929–1931

140

ERIC MENDELSOHN

GERMAN METAL WORKERS'
UNION BUILDING
BERLIN, GERMANY, 1929–1930

E. GUNNAR ASPLUND   STOCKHOLM EXHIBITION OF 1930   STOCKHOLM, SWEDEN, 1930

HOOD & HOWELLS   DAILY NEWS BUILDING   NEW YORK, NEW YORK, 1930

144

HOWE & LESCAZE

PHILADELPHIA SAVINGS FUND SOCIETY
PHILADELPHIA, PENNSYLVANIA, 1931-1932

145

REINHARD, HOFMEISTER, B. W. MORRIS, CORBETT, HARMON & MAC MURRAY, HOOD AND FOUILHOUX
ROCKEFELLER CENTER   NEW YORK, NEW YORK, 1931–1937

146

. . . ROCKEFELLER CENTER   NEW YORK

149

SUTEMI HORIGUCHI   OKADA HOUSE   TOKYO, JAPAN, 1934

GIUSEPPE TERRAGNI   CASA DEL POPOLO   COMO, ITALY, 1932–1936

LUIGI FIGINI AND GINO POLLINI

NURSERY SCHOOL AT OLIVETTI TYPEWRITER FACTORY   IVREA, ITALY, 1935–1945

TECTON GROUP   HIGHPOINT FLATS   LONDON, ENGLAND, 1936–1938

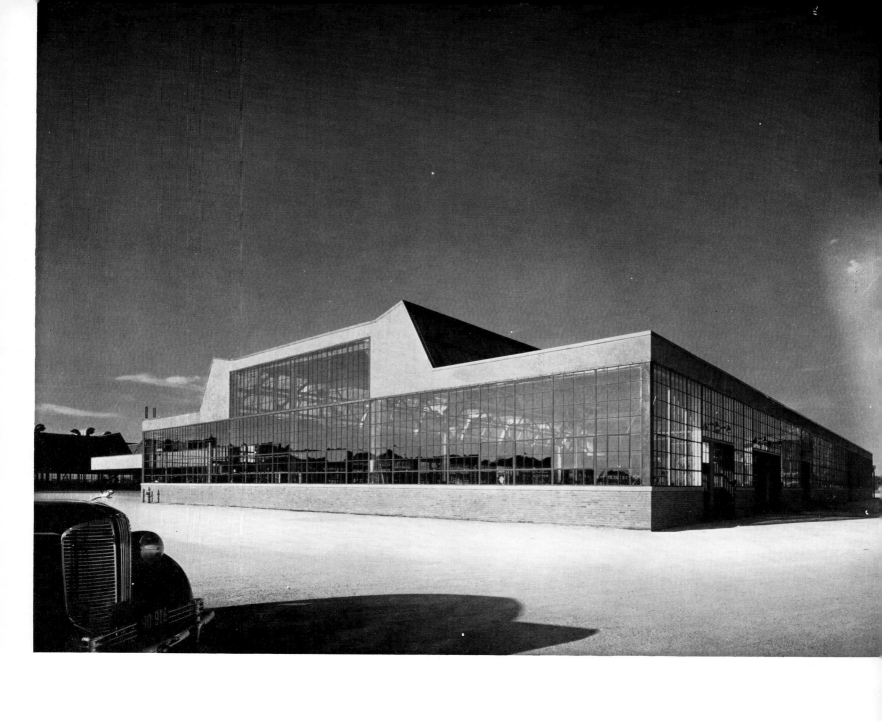

ALBERT KAHN   DODGE TRUCK PLANT   DETROIT, MICHIGAN, 1938

ARNE JACOBSEN   AARHUS TOWN HALL   DENMARK, 1939–1942

TECTON GROUP   PENGUIN POOL, REGENT'S PARK ZOO   LONDON, ENGLAND, 1938

158

MARCEL AND MILTON ROBERTO   SANTOS DUMONT AIRPORT   RIO DE JANEIRO, BRAZIL, 1940

LUCIO COSTA   APARTMENT HOUSES   RIO DE JANEIRO, BRAZIL, 1947–1953

AFFONSO REIDY   APARTMENT HOUSES AND SCHOOL   RIO DE JANEIRO, BRAZIL, 1948–1950

CHARLES EAMES

CASE STUDY HOUSE
SANTA MONICA, CALIFORNIA, 1949

PHILIP JOHNSON   PHILIP JOHNSON HOUSE   NEW CANAAN, CONNECTICUT, 1949

L. CALINI (ENGINEER), E. MONTUORI, M. CASTELLAZZI,
V. FADIGATI, A. PINTONELLO, A. VITELLOZZI
ROME RAILROAD TERMINAL   ROME, ITALY, 1950

PIETRO BELLUSCHI   FIRST PRESBYTERIAN CHURCH   COTTAGE GROVE, OREGON, 1950

WALLACE K. HARRISON, ARCHITECT IN CHARGE
UNITED NATIONS SECRETARIAT BUILDING   NEW YORK, NEW YORK, 1950

PAUL RUDOLPH AND RALPH S. TWITCHELL   W. R. HEALY HOUSE   SARASOTA, FLORIDA, 1950

HARWELL H. HARRIS

RALPH JOHNSON HOUSE
LOS ANGELES, CALIFORNIA, 1951

JUNZO SAKAKURA   MUSEUM OF MODERN ART   KAMAKURA, JAPAN, 1951

JUAN O'GORMAN, GUSTAVO SAAVODRA AND JUAN MARTINEZ DE VALESCO

UNIVERSITY CITY OF MEXICO LIBRARY
MEXICO CITY, MEXICO, 1951–1953

KENZO TANGE   MEMORIAL PEACE CENTER   HIROSHIMA, JAPAN, 1951

DONALD BARTHELME & ASSOCIATES

WEST COLUMBIA ELEMENTARY SCHOOL
WEST COLUMBIA, TEXAS, 1952

180

HARRISON & ABRAMOVITZ

ALCOA BUILDING
PITTSBURGH, PENNSYLVANIA, 1952

181

SKIDMORE, OWINGS AND MERRILL

LEVER HOUSE   NEW YORK, NEW YORK, 1952

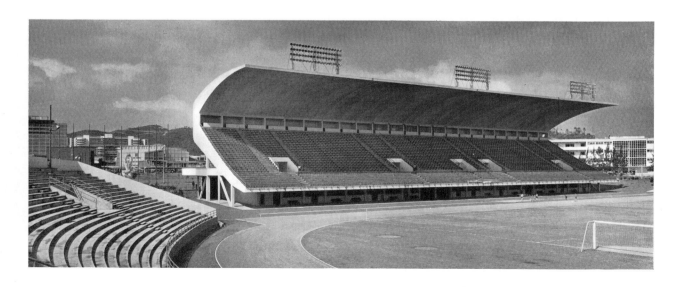

CARLOS VILLANUEVA

CARACAS UNIVERSITY CITY
CARACAS, VENEZUELA, 1952–1953

OSVALDO BRATKE   BRATKE HOUSE   SAO PAULO, BRAZIL, 1953

186

LONDON COUNTY COUNCIL

ROEHAMPTON BUILDING
LONDON, ENGLAND, 1953

187

ANTONIN RAYMOND & L. L. RADO   U.S. EMBASSY HOUSING   TOKYO, JAPAN, 1954

ELIOT NOYES   ELIOT NOYES HOUSE   NEW CANAAN, CONNECTICUT, 1954

SKIDMORE, OWINGS AND MERRILL

MANUFACTURERS TRUST COMPANY   NEW YORK, NEW YORK, 1954

YAMASAKI, HELLMUTH & LEINWEBER
LAMBERT-ST. LOUIS AIRPORT   ST. LOUIS, MISSOURI, 1954

I. M. PEI

MILE HIGH CENTER
DENVER, COLORADO, 1955

LONDON COUNTY COUNCIL; J. L. MARTIN, DESIGNER

CATFORD SECONDARY SCHOOL
LONDON, ENGLAND, 1955

SKIDMORE, OWINGS AND MERRILL

CONNECTICUT GENERAL LIFE INSURANCE COMPANY   BLOOMFIELD, CONNECTICUT, 1957

... CONNECTICUT GENERAL LIFE INSURANCE COMPANY   BLOOMFIELD, CONNECTICUT

Building Descriptions

41   UNITY TEMPLE. Frank Lloyd Wright. Oak Park, Illinois, 1906. This building was Wright's
      and America's first important structure built of poured concrete. The pebble aggregate was
exposed in order to relieve the plainness of the surface and the doubts of the clients. A massive,
square building with an auditorium raised above its surrounding corridors, the church is notable
for its complex interior spatial relationships.

42-43   AVERY COONLEY HOUSE. Frank Lloyd Wright. Riverside, Illinois, 1908. The principal areas
         of this house are almost-independent pavilions. The living room pavilion dominates the
main façade and faces an intricate arrangement of terrace and reflecting pool. Especially noteworthy
in this building is the richness of the exterior decorations. The upper story is ornamented
with colored tiles, which are supplemented by lines cut into the surface plaster.

44-45   FREDERICK C. ROBIE HOUSE. Frank Lloyd Wright. Chicago, Illinois, 1909. This early Wright
         house is one of the most celebrated residences in modern architecture. Visually a series of
exciting planes, this brick house is lined with balconies. The living floor is raised and in its linear arrangement is suggestive of an ocean liner. The decklike appearance of the balconies enhances the
low horizontal look.

46-47   TALIESIN. Frank Lloyd Wright. Spring Green, Wisconsin, 1914. Taliesin, the home of a
         great master, is a great masterpiece. It is not a building but a complex of houses, studios,
farm, and school, built, and twice rebuilt, around a hilltop overlooking the rolling Wisconsin farm-
lands The site, the landscaping, the wide use of natural materials, and the great sweeping roofs make
this eastern home photograph less dramatically than Wright's winter encampment in the Arizona
desert, Taliesin West. But architecture is an art of space. The rooms of Taliesin are second to none.
The living room, for example, is considered by many to be Wright's finest domestic interior. Filled
with superb works of oriental art, Taliesin is itself a brilliant work of the art of architecture.

48   GEORGE MADISON MILLARD HOUSE. Frank Lloyd Wright. Pasadena, California, 1923. Wright's
      concern for the integration of building and setting is perfectly exemplified in this unusual
house, one of his first "block" houses. It is situated at the bottom of a ravine, amid luxuriant plant-
ings, and is three stories high. The two-story living room is entered at the second-floor level; the
dining room is on the floor below and opens onto the terrace.

49   CHARLES ENNIS HOUSE. Frank Lloyd Wright. Los Angeles, California, 1924. This massive house rises from one of the Hollywood hills; its weight and dignity have been said to give it the appearance of a public monument—specifically, a Mayan one. It is surrounded by an enormous terrace that enhances the impression. This house is a striking example of textile-block construction combining metal rods with precast concrete blocks.

50-51   "FALLING WATER," EDGAR J. KAUFMANN HOUSE. Frank Lloyd Wright. Bear Run, Pennsylvania, 1936. Here is a flawless meeting of architecture and engineering—the most famous house in modern architecture. The great cantilevered slabs of this house on a waterfall seem to grow out of the rock itself. Masonry constructed of the native stone contrasts vigorously with the smooth concrete of the slabs. Because of the cantilever construction, the walls are only screens of glass opening out to the wooded surroundings.

52-53   S. C. JOHNSON & SON, INC., BUILDINGS. Frank Lloyd Wright. Racine, Wisconsin, 1936–1939. The most famous feature of the administration building is the slender concrete "lily pad" piers which emphasize the interior space and combine at their tops to form the ceiling. The exterior walls are brick screens striated with bands of glass tubing, with interior walls of plate glass. The near by fourteen-story research tower is enclosed in a similar "glass envelope," and its floors are supported by a single central shaft.

54-57   TALIESIN WEST. Frank Lloyd Wright. Paradise Valley, near Phoenix, Arizona, 1938–. Winter headquarters for the Taliesin Fellowship, this remarkable creation consists of a base of purplish-red desert-stone blocks set in concrete topped by a tentlike superstructure. This superstructure is of canvas supported by dramatic timber trusses. The entire camp seems a natural, unique part of its colorful desert setting. The unsurpassed handling of light and space makes it one of the most celebrated buildings in modern architecture.

58-59   ROSE PAUSON HOUSE. Frank Lloyd Wright. Phoenix, Arizona, 1940. With its base of canted purple fieldstone blocks, surmounted by a wooden superstructure, this house is strongly reminiscent of Taliesin West. It is situated on a desert knoll, and the living room's French doors open on a striking view. Simple in composition, the house is of special interest because of the careful way in which wood and masonry elements are related.

60-61   H. C. PRICE TOWER. Frank Lloyd Wright. Bartlesville, Oklahoma, 1953–1956. Rising 186 feet above the Oklahoma plain, this spectacular building is Wright's first residential skyscraper. Its exterior colors are brilliant—blue-green copper fins and facings, golden-tinted windows. Each floor is divided into quadrants, three of them devoted to offices and one comprising a vertical half of a duplex apartment.

62   SINGLE HOUSE FOR THE STUTTGART EXHIBITION. Le Corbusier. Stuttgart, Germany, 1927. The housing exhibition at Stuttgart, supervised by Mies van der Rohe, was one of the most important events in modern architecture between the two world wars This four-story, rectangular building is one of the three houses designed by Le Corbusier for the exhibition at Mies van der Rohe's request. The elevating pillars begin as circles on the ground floor and become squares on the upper floors. The southern exposure has large windows, while the other walls are primarily solid. As is characteristic of Le Corbusier's work, the concrete skeleton allows the free placement of the non-supporting inner walls.

63   SAVOYE HOUSE. Le Corbusier and Pierre Jeanneret. Poissy-sur-Seine, France, 1928–1930. In
the Savoye House, built on an isolated site in the beautiful Seine Valley, Le Corbusier realized his five central principles of architecture: free standing pillars, framework designed so that the
skeleton and walls are functionally independent of each other, open planning, freedom and variation
of interior spaces, free façade, and a flat roof which could be used as a garden. The house, designed
as a cube elevated on pillars, has an open view on all sides and large areas of glass enabling its ten-
ants to look out upon the surrounding landscape. It relates man to his environment in a manner
that has made it one of the most influential houses in modern architecture.

64-65   SWISS DORMITORY, CITÉ UNIVERSITAIRE. Le Corbusier. Paris, France, 1930–1932. Charac-
teristically, this pavilion of Le Corbusier's is elevated on huge concrete pillars and is provided on one side with an elegant glass curtain wall. Another wall of the structure is constructed on a
curved plan, the lower portion being designed of stones left in their natural shapes. In striking contrast, the upper portion of this same wall is constructed of smooth, uniform, white concrete slabs. The
organization of the building's interior realizes Le Corbusier's principle of *le plan libre:* The pillars, the
curved partitions, and the winding staircase are organized independently of each other. When
viewed as a whole, however, the free and individualized spaces and forms combine to form a distinct aesthetic unity.

66-69   UNITÉ D'HABITATION. Le Corbusier, Marseilles, France, 1943–1950. This great rectangular
slab, designed to house 1000 people, is a frame of ferroconcrete into which apartment
units are prefabricated and quite literally inserted. Almost all of these apartments are two stories
high, with full-length balconies and expanses of window. Le Corbusier's familiar *brise-soleil* protects
the occupants from excessive sun. On the roof, which is public, are a swimming pool, a solarium, and
a running track.

70-73   CHAPEL OF NOTRE DAME-DU-HAUT. Le Corbusier. Ronchamp, France, 1950–1955. The
sculptured forms and spaces of this extraordinary chapel are the recognized work of a
master. A narrow space between the roof shell and the walls allows light to enter; in addition there is
a system of windows, some clear, some of glazed glass. The towers are of stone and are capped by
cement domes. The walls—both inside and out—are surfaced with whitewashed mortar. Color
contrast is created inside by the dramatic use of deep red and purple.

74-77   HIGH COURT BUILDING. Le Corbusier, with Pierre Jeanneret, E. Maxwell Fry, and Jane
Drew. Chandigarh, India, 1957–. Rising from the dusty Punjab plain is a new capital
city, one of the largest and most celebrated complexes of modern architecture. Its government
center is dominated by this building, which presents a series of gigantic sculptured forms. A huge
cantilevered roof, suggesting a parasol, offers protection from both sun and monsoon rains. A lobby
and ramps lead from the open entrance to the courtrooms. Offices are at the rear of the building.

78-79   GERMAN PAVILION AT THE INTERNATIONAL EXPOSITION. Ludwig Mies van der Rohe.
Barcelona, Spain, 1929. Mies's most famous European achievement unfortunately stood
for only one year, since it was designed for the Barcelona Exposition of 1929. Constructed of steel
columns and rectangular planes used as walls and roof, it gave an effect of flowing, unlimited
spaciousness. The architect gave this pure and precise modern building an air of opulence by the
use of rich materials.

80-81   TUGENDHAT HOUSE. Ludwig Mies van der Rohe. Brno, Czechoslovakia, 1930. Mies here
created what has been called a modern classic. The huge main space is divided into four
rooms, or areas, defined by a straight wall of onyx and a curved one of ebony. The spaciousness is en-
hanced by the two outside walls, which are completely of glass. Every detail was designed by the
architect with remarkable style and precision.

82-85 CAMPUS, ILLINOIS INSTITUTE OF TECHNOLOGY. Ludwig Mies van der Rohe. Chicago, Illinois, 1939–. Notable in many respects, this enormous project is especially significant because it is one of the largest group plans by any modern architect. The arrangement of buildings in a series of plazas is simple but subtle. Every building is based on a common bay. This modular principle exerts a strong unifying effect. The Library and Administration Building, considered by some critics to be Mies's finest work, is a huge 300 × 200 × 300 foot rectangle. Structural elements are completely exposed, and one section contains a 22-foot vertical space interrupted only by a large mezzanine cantilevered from central columns.

86-87 EDITH FARNSWORTH HOUSE. Ludwig Mies van der Rohe. Plano, Illinois, 1950. Continuous, visible space is the essence of this house, which is fundamentally a wall of glass stretched between two horizontal planes—the roof and the raised floor. Eight steel columns keep the two planes suspended. Bathrooms, kitchen, and service facilities are contained in a wood-sheathed enclosure placed at one side of the principal room.

88-89 860 LAKE SHORE DRIVE APARTMENT HOUSES. Ludwig Mies van der Rohe. Chicago, Illinois, 1951. Probably the most distinctive apartment buildings in the United States, these twin towers enjoy a sweeping view of the city and Lake Michigan. The exterior walls are totally of glass, constructed in a steel frame. Steel beams serve as both window mullions and decorations emphasizing the linear quality of the buildings. To ensure uniformity of appearance, every apartment is equipped with identical gray shades. In daylight, the total effect is that of a huge mirror.

90 SEAGRAM BUILDING. Ludwig Mies van der Rohe and Philip Johnson. New York, New York, 1958. This Manhattan office building is a master statement expressing the skyscraper's essentially cage-like structure directly and dramatically. Set back on a marble and granite plaza, the thirty-eight story tower is flanked by two low wings which provide a backdrop and accentuate the impression of sheer height. The simple geometry of the building's module carried from top to bottom gives it unsurpassed unity and rhythm. The bronze-sheathed steel frame, warm tinted glass and polished travertine provide a richness that heightens the building's simplicity and precision.

91 FAGUS WORKS. Walter Gropius. Alfeld, Germany, 1911. This shoe factory, of cantilevered skeleton construction, marks a use of the steel frame that was unprecedented in 1911. The walls are free-standing glass curtains emphasized by the lack of corner columns. Gropius' first large building, this purely industrial structure remains a remarkable achievement and a landmark in the development of modern architecture.

92 BAUHAUS. Walter Gropius. Dessau, Germany, 1926. The Bauhaus was a complete school, with auditorium, dormitory, canteen, and offices in addition to departments and workshops. In this building complex, Gropius separated these elements while still integrating them into a whole. In its basic plan the Bauhaus is two large L's that intersect each other at various levels; the arm of one L is a bridge over the street. The most famous feature of the group is the glass curtain walls of the Bauhaus building itself.

93 MUNICIPAL EMPLOYMENT OFFICE. Walter Gropius. Dessau, Germany, 1928. Gropius' first office building owes its semicircular plan to the economic situation at the time. To enable officials to handle large numbers of unemployed workers of different occupations, Gropius placed separate entrances for each trade around the periphery, with consultation rooms at the center. The inner rooms are lit by glass ceilings. At one side the semicircle is prolonged to form a bicycle shed.

94-95 LOVELL HOUSE. Richard J. Neutra. Los Angeles, California, 1929. An early believer in the "airy, light skeleton" building, Neutra achieved precisely that effect here: Wide openings and large windows almost literally bring the outdoors inside. The building, of light steel construction, rises two stories above a hillside and has full southern exposure. The walls, of reinforced concrete, were applied by air compression.

96 SALGINATOBEL BRIDGE. Robert Maillart. Switzerland, 1929–1930. The Salginatobel Bridge, near Schiers, Graubünden, is Maillart's widest arch—a 90-meter span and 132 meters in length. The low, hollow arch has vertical supports between it and the platform. In the midst of a tremendous rugged mountain landscape, it seems to soar almost immaterially over the steep gorge.

97 THE SCHWANDBACH BRIDGE. Robert Maillart. Berne, Switzerland, 1933. This is considered one of the purest and most striking of all Maillart's bridges. Spanning a deep ravine, the bridge curves gently to follow the bending roadway. The stiffened arch lifts the highway across the chasm with an unexcelled economy of means.

98 BRIDGE OVER THE RIVER THUR. Robert Maillart. Near St. Galli, Switzerland, 1933. Like a great piece of modern sculpture, this bridge crosses the river Thur at Henau-Uzwil. The bridge deck rests on twin hollow ribs economically made with the same building forms. Here for the first time, Maillart used the pointed arch, creating a bridge which seems hardly to touch the ground.

99 DOLDERTHAL APARTMENTS. Marcel Breuer and Alfred and Émil Roth. Zurich, Switzerland, 1934. This group of apartment houses, Breuer's last prewar work on the Continent, exemplifies his concern for the relationship between buildings and nature. Each building contains three apartments and two penthouses; on every floor a terrace offers the equivalent of a garden. In the lobby an indoor-outdoor planting bed, uninterrupted by the glass wall, creates continuity with the world outside.

100-101 EXPERIMENTAL SCHOOL. Richard J. Neutra. Los Angeles, California, 1934–1935. Designed for activity rather than simply for listening, a concept that has since become common, this school is essentially a collection of individual classroom units. Each has its own "outdoor schoolroom." With corridors eliminated, the rooms have windows on both sides. Neutra cautiously described the building at the time as a "restricted" experiment, but it has become one of the most influential school buildings in the United States.

102-103 HIPPODROME. Eduardo Torroja. Madrid, Spain, 1935. The roof canopies over the grandstands of the Madrid racetrack are barrel-shaped shells of reinforced concrete cantilevered out 42 feet over the stepped seat sections. The individual impression of each shell and the cumulative effect of all the shells viewed in a sweep are remarkable for lightness and strength.

104-105   BRIDGE OVER THE RIVER ARVE. Robert Maillart. Switzerland, 1936–1937. This celebrated roadbridge over a river in the gentle valley of Vessey Genève is very different from the stark soaring beauty of Maillart's mountain bridges. It is noteworthy for its aesthetic perfection and the technical ingenuity of Maillart's triple three-hinge arch, a wide, slightly pointed arch with the supports reduced to the statically permitted minimum.

106-107   THE MINISTRY OF EDUCATION AND HEALTH. Lucio Costa, Oscar Niemeyer, Affonso Reidy, Carlos Leao, Jorge Moreira, and Hernani Vasconcelos (Le Corbusier, consultant). Rio de Janeiro, 1937–1943. Designed for civic benefit and beauty by a selected group of Brazilian architects, this great building houses fifteen floors of offices, an amphitheater, and exhibition halls. Wall surfaces are varied both in texture and color: rose granite, blue and white ceramic tile, uninterrupted windows, and a huge sunshade. Candido Portinari's tile mural, a high relief on the amphitheater's façade by Jacques Lipchitz and sculptures by Berino Giorgio and Antonio Celso in the beautifully landscaped garden are outstanding examples of the integration of related arts.

108-110   SUNILA FACTORY (HOUSES AND PULP MILLS). Alvar Aalto. Finland, 1937–1939. The largest cellulose factory in Finland is on a small elevated island near the eastern shore of Kotka and dominates the seascape like a modern-day cathedral. Long lines of conveyor belts feed the logs from the river mouth and discharge the bales to the harbor. A vaulted warehouse is turned towards the harbor. Nearby workers' houses and administration buildings are part of Aalto's unified plan for the whole area.

111   TABERNACLE CHURCH OF CHRIST. Eliel and Eero Saarinen. Columbus, Indiana, 1938–1942. One of the most challenging architectural commissions today is a modern church. The Tabernacle Church of Christ, designed by modern architecture's most famous father and son team is a completely contemporary building that honors ancient spiritual traditions, at the same time that it provides for newer social functions. In general plan and style it is an excellent example of the work of the elder Saarinen in America.

112-113   MILITARY HANGARS. Pier Luigi Nervi. Orbitello, Italy, 1938–1942. The great engineer among contemporary builders, Nervi is best known for the amazingly diverse uses to which he has put reinforced concrete—and the unity of structure and form that became possible as a result of his work. The first of these hangars, with its lamella-type framing, was poured on the site, but by 1942 Nervi had developed precasting, which made possible a great saving of critical materials.

114-115   CHAMBERLAIN HOUSE. Walter Gropius and Marcel Breuer. Sudbury, Massachusetts, 1939. With its enclosed porch, this widely admired house is cruciform in shape. The main floor, which is frame, perches on a substructure of local stone. The construction is strutted frame and the siding is of oiled redwood. In its simplicity this modern house is in keeping with the oldest traditions of New England building.

116-117   CHURCH OF ST. FRANCIS OF ASSISI. Oscar Neimeyer. Pampulha, Brazil, 1943. This controversial modern church is a dramatic example of the new ecclesiastical architecture. The tall vault of the high altar is flanked on either side by two smaller vaults—the transepts. For this five-arch space on the rear wall, Portinari has designed a predominantly blue tile mural of the life of St. Francis. Inside, behind the high altar, is a companion mural of Christ forgiving and healing. The use of ceramic tile is in keeping with an ancient Iberian tradition which now enriches much South American modern architecture.

118-119   CHANNEL HEIGHTS HOUSING PROJECT. Richard J. Neutra. San Pedro, California, 1943–
1944. A federal, public housing authority project for San Pedro shipworkers, Channel
Heights is built on a rugged 165-acre California site of hills, ravines, and canyons. There are four
different types of houses to accommodate 600 families of different sizes and tastes. The living quarters
of each house face the ocean. Most of the buildings are one story and are constructed of prefabricated
parts. Facades are mainly of durable California redwood and cement plaster. The project is a self-
contained community including a school, playgrounds, a well-landscaped public park, a community
center, administration offices, a firehouse, and a shopping center. Neutra had succeeded in disprov-
ing the common notion that mass low-cost housing can have no individuality or style.

120-121   ROBINSON HOUSE. Marcel Breuer. Williamstown, Massachusetts, 1946. Here is this architect's "binuclear" plan at work: The H design permits the house to be divided into two
distinct areas, one for daytime living, one for night. An entrance hall links the two and faces one of
the patios created by the floor plan. This hall likewise serves as a ramp bridging the two floor levels.

122-123   KAUFMANN RESIDENCE. Richard J. Neutra. Palm Springs, California, 1947. Here the outdoors is related to the interior in two ways: Outdoor space is included in the plan, and
the desert landscape is present in numerous striking vistas. The design is open, with four wings. A
sheltered porch protects the living room from the sun; additional protection from the weather, including sandstorms, is provided by vertical aluminum blinds.

124   TURIN EXHIBITION HALL. Pier Luigi Nervi. Turin, Italy, 1947–1950. As a part of his work with
precasting Nervi developed "ferrocement," which consists of layers of fine wire mesh em-
bedded in cement mortar. This material made possible this exhibition hall's famous shell. Here the
prefabricated sections, only 1½ inches thick, formed the striking curve of the vault.

125   SALT WAREHOUSE. Pier Luigi Nervi. Tortona, Italy, 1950. Nervi's remarkable engineering
imagination here provides a unique shelter for bulk salt fed from a neighboring building.
The 39-foot high warehouse consists of 27 parabolic arches of reinforced concrete, which carry inter-
mediate vaults of precast concrete spans. The beauty of this utilitarian building called architectural
attention to the aesthetic qualities of reinforced concrete.

126-127   HARVARD UNIVERSITY GRADUATE CENTER. The Architects' Collaborative. Cambridge,
Massachusetts, 1949–1950. Seven dormitories and a commons building are designed
around a series of quadrangles as important to the total composition as the buildings themselves.
Two and three stories in height, the dormitories are of reinforced concrete construction. The commons is a one-story curved building with a steel skeleton. Walter Gropius and his associates have
here created a modern campus building that honors traditional collegiate planning.

128-129   GENERAL MOTORS TECHNICAL CENTER. Eero Saarinen. Detroit, Michigan, 1951-1957. This gleaming complex of 25 buildings suggests the ultimate in industrial architecture. Here, in this remarkable concentration of buildings, are housed the research facilities of the world's largest corporation. The exterior materials—aluminum, stainless steel, glass, and porcelain enamel —give an effect of machine-like precision. Brilliantly hued walls of ceramic glazed brick enliven efficiency with bright color. Courts, gardens, and pools, designed for the delight of the employees, reaffirm the human element.

130-131   NIEMEYER HOUSE. Oscar Niemeyer. Rio de Janeiro, Brazil, 1953-1954. This house is a striking South American example of modern residential architecture. The pavilion containing the living areas and kitchen is openly constructed to provide a view of the ocean and surrounding trees and hills. The serpentine shapes of the roof and swimming pool form a distinctly modern and imaginative design. The stark whiteness of the building materials contrasts effectively with the muted greens and browns of the structure's natural surroundings.

132–133   MASSACHUSETTS INSTITUTE OF TECHNOLOGY, KRESGE AUDITORIUM AND CHAPEL. Eero Saarinen. Cambridge, Massachusetts, 1955. This domed auditorium and cylindrical chapel represent a courageous effort by one of America's leading architects to free modern buildings from box-like forms. The auditorium is a thin shell concrete dome spanning 155 feet. Its 1500 tons rest at three points like a huge spinnacker on a grassy M.I.T. terrace. In contrast, the form of the chapel was determined from within, where the curved walls, reflected light and striking sculpture create a chapel designed for individual meditation.

134-135   TECHNICAL INSTITUTE OF CONCRETE CONSTRUCTION. Eduardo Torroja with M. Barbero and G. Echegaray. Madrid, Spain, 1955. In this concrete technical institute, for which Eduardo Torroja is director and designer, concrete is used in a purposeful variety of shapes. A driveway, flanked by flat-vaulted laboratories on one side and a parking lot on the other, leads to the main office building. The most compelling constructions on this road are the dodecahedron coal bunker and chimney, raised like statues on a round pedestal. Among the many other noteworthy structures are the circular restaurant built in a mushroom shape with cantilevered roof, the 18-foot centilevered pergola frames at the edge of the parking lot.

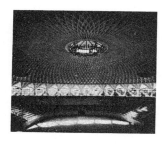

136   OLYMPIC SPORTS PALACE. Pier Luigi Nervi, engineer, Annibale Vitellozzi, architect. Rome, Italy, 1957. This 5,000 seat sports stadium has a roof recognized as a triumph of art and engineering. 1,620 pre-cast concrete sections were set in a form and bound together into a reinforced concrete dome. The dome spans some 194 feet and rests lightly on 36 Y-shaped piers. From inside, Nervi's delicately ribbed structure has a beauty fashioned with the imagination of a modern mathematician and the honesty of a master builder.

137   WORKERS' HOUSES. J. J. P. Oud. Hook of Holland, Holland, 1926-1927. These simple, two-story, row houses with flat roofs are outstanding examples of early modern architecture. They are arranged in two continuous sections, with a sweeping terrace running through. The verticality of the ramp of the terrace, curved on both ends, is a central feature. White walls, yellow brick foundations, gray bands, and bluish ironwork add to the delicacy and originality of the design.

138   VAN NELLE TOBACCO, TEA, AND COFFEE FACTORY. Brinkman and van der Vlugt. Rotterdam, Holland, 1928-1930. One of the pioneer designs in factory planning is this group of warehouses, offices, garages, and canteens outside Rotterdam. The main factory building is an eight-story mushroom slab of reinforced concrete with glass curtain walls, light and translucent, in spite of the inherent solidity of the whole design. Deliberate variations in this design are made in the buildings according to their functions.

139   SCHOCKEN DEPARTMENT STORE. Eric Mendelsohn. Chemnitz, Germany, 1928–1930. Considered Mendelsohn's masterpiece, the nine-story Schocken Department Store covers an
irregular site: two streets joining a curved, main avenue. Its shape is a sector of a circle, the
circumference forming the 220-foot façade. Broad horizontal window bands of uninterrupted glass
are equally impressive in daylight and when lit up at night. The three upper stories are recessed,
and large vertical windows on each end of the building mark the staircases.

140   TOWN HALL. Willem Dudok. Hilversum, Holland, 1929–1931. A renowned pioneer of the
modern movement, Dudok achieved a "cubistic triumph" in this town hall, designed in
1924. The bright brickwork is almost festive, and the entire building has the warmth that is characteristic of this architect's work. The offices are arranged along passages around an inner court,
with the entrances at the rear of the building. The front entrance is reserved for high officials
and, uniquely, bridal parties.

141   GERMAN METAL WORKERS' UNION BUILDING. Eric Mendelsohn. Berlin, Germany, 1929-1930.
This was the only part of Mendelsohn's great town planning scheme for Berlin that was
executed. Built on a triangular site formed by the juncture of two streets, the reinforced concrete
structure has a sector-like plan and concave façade. Contributing to the flowing monumentality
that Mendelsohn has achieved here are the long horizontal bands of windows accentuated by
bronze frames and the famous circular staircase inside.

142-143   STOCKHOLM EXHIBITION OF 1930. Gunnar Asplund. Stockholm, Sweden, 1930. Gunnar
Asplund was the chief architect of the 1930 Stockholm Exhibition, an experimental
project to provide the layman with his first chance to view modern architecture in the appropriate
modern setting rather than in incongruous surroundings. Before this, expositions customarily dis-
played fantastic or bizarre architecture. Asplund's innovation at Stockholm has emphasized the
architect's role of serving the community at large. The Paradisit Restaurant at the exhibition was
designed by Asplund himself, an elegant realization of the exhibition's philosophy: the architectural harmonizing of form and function.

144   DAILY NEWS BUILDING. Hood & Howells. New York, New York, 1930. One of New
York's most distinguished skyscrapers, the Daily News Building is designed with a vertical
emphasis. This tall feeling is achieved by the soaring asymmetrical contours and by the facade in
which bands of white brick wall are alternated with unbroken bands of window glass and dark
spandrel. The roof area with utilities is concealed behind several story-heights of wall.

145   PHILADELPHIA SAVINGS FUND SOCIETY. Howe and Lescaze. Philadelphia, Pennsylvania,
1931-1932. In this celebrated skyscraper design, a T-shaped plan above the fifth floor of
this thirty-three-story building provides maximum daylight. The floors are cantilevered beyond the
supporting columns to provide walls in which bands of glass alternate with light gray brick. A large
marble entrance hall with an enormous glass window leads to the second floor main banking area.
Elevators are concentrated in one block of glazed black brick.

146-149   ROCKEFELLER CENTER. Reinhard, Hofmeister, B. W. Morris, Corbett, Harmon and
            MacMurray, Hood and Fouilhoux. New York, New York, 1931-1937. This group of
skyscrapers, planned as a unified office and entertainment center, is simple in architectural design
and highly imaginative in urban approach. The great slab of the central building dominates one
of the first and most dramatic modern civic centers. The huge buildings are grouped around a
fountained plaza and a small garden. The interiors are enriched by the allied arts of painting,
sculpture, and mosaics. Here the American skyscraper has found a superb setting.

150   CASA DEL POPOLO. Giuseppe Terragni. Como, Italy, 1932-1936. This building, begun in
        1932 and completed four years later, is one of the early Italian modern designs with ad-
mirably rational plan and straightforward handling of materials. Just as the architect's Day Nur-
ery School at Como, Italy, is considered the finest modern Italian school, so the Casa del Popolo
is considered by many to be the most outstanding modern public building in all of Italy.

151   OKADA HOUSE. Sutemi Horiguchi. Tokyo, Japan, 1934. In this influential house, one of
        Japan's leading architects has effectively combined traditional Eastern and modern West-
ern architectural styles. Built in almost classic relationship to its natural surroundings, the living
room of the house looks out upon a rectangular pool as well as a series of gardens surrounded by
concrete walls. One of the most striking traditional features of the Okada House is its terrace constructed of horizontally laid bamboo strips contrasting with the horizontal planes of pool and garden walls. The sensitive use of stones and plants as well as building materials demonstrates the
oriental relationship between indoor and outdoor space.

152   NURSERY SCHOOL AT OLIVETTI TYPEWRITER FACTORY. Luigi Figini and Gino Pollini. Ivrea,
        Italy, 1935-1945. A nursery school with prenatal clinic forms part of the socially advanced
workers' housing of the Olivetti typewriter factory. A two-story building harmoniously set into a
mountain landscape relates the design of the building nearby. Precast concrete beams and rough-
faced stone walling are handled with refined skill.

153   HIGHPOINT FLATS. The Tecton Group. London, England, 1936-1938. The Highpoint Flats,
        an eight-story building of reinforced concrete, is one of the milestones of modern architec-
ture in England. Each of the 60 middle-income apartments has a cross-shaped plan to allow for
compactness and the maximum of sunlight. Cantilevered balconies and long glass windows
emphasize the vertical on the facade.

154-155   DODGE TRUCK PLANT. Albert Kahn. Detroit, Michigan, 1938. This group of buildings,
            an assembly building 1260 feet long, a railway shipping dock, and an export build-
ing, is considered by experts to be one of the most perfect examples of American modern factory
design. The cantilevered roof trusses of the assembly building, the wonderful use of glass on the
export building and the characteristic combination of welding and riveting in the supporting
structures are noteworthy features.

156   PENGUIN POOL, REGENT'S PARK ZOO. The Tecton Group. London, England, 1938. This is an example of excellent modern architecture in an unusual place. Like a huge modern sculpture, two cantilevered ramps spiral around each other over an elliptical pool. The whole is surrounded by a low perforated wall.

157   AARHUS TOWN HALL. Arne Jacobsen. Denmark, 1939-1942. A main block including offices, reception hall, marriage hall, and council hall forms the remarkable municipal center for Denmark's second largest city. The roofs of two administration wings are flatly curved and the open frame tower has a huge clock. The structure is faced with gray-blue reinforced concrete and Norwegian marble.

158-159   CROW ISLAND SCHOOL. Eliel and Eero Saarinen with Perkins, Wheeler and Will. Winnetka, Illinois, 1939-1940. Planning for a friendly and free environment, the architects have placed one-story school buildings for each age group in a free arrangement around the central office and library section. Based on the new curriculum, Crow Island School is widely regarded as the most influential modern school in America.

160   SANTOS DUMONT AIRPORT. Marcel and Milton Roberto. Rio de Janeiro, Brazil, 1940. The main building of this large airport is the passenger terminal, a long four-story structure of reinforced concrete built on massive piles cast in place. Its western facade is covered by a delicate *brise-soleil*. The ground floor is designed for passenger services and shops, the mezzanine for restaurants and airline facilities, the two top floors for administration. A separate wing houses meteorological and communications services.

161   APARTMENT HOUSES. Lucio Costa. Rio de Janeiro, Brazil, 1947-1953. A beautiful landscape of trees, rocks, and varied terrain provides an unusual rural setting for this group of Brazilian apartment houses. The individual buildings are relatively low to maintain a human scale. The sun-louver pattern is designed to outline the apartments as individual units, thus avoiding an impression of anonymity. The light, gleaming colors of the building façade make the structures the focal point of their surrounding tropical landscape.

162-163   APARTMENT HOUSES AND SCHOOLS. Affonso Reidy. Rio de Janeiro, Brazil, 1948-1950. This group of low-cost apartments unified with community center and school is set dramatically on a hill. The big block of the curved main building is entered midway up the hill by a bridge. Tile grilles for sun control, painted stucco, and blue tile (azulejos) decorate the façades. Strong horizontal bands organize the building in rectangular areas. Roofed by a low-pitched shell vault, the school has a classroom wing on the side slope and a small gymnasium, decorated in front with Portinari's azulejo murals.

164-165   CASE STUDY HOUSE. Charles Eames. Santa Monica, California, 1949. Prototype of modern building, this house was designed by Eames of standard industrial components. All of the building elements are mass-produced: The walls consist chiefly of steel windows and sliding glass doors. Contrast is provided by solid panels of red, white, or blue. The bedrooms open onto a mezzanine overlooking the high-ceilinged living room.

166-167   PHILIP JOHNSON HOUSE. Philip Johnson. New Canaan, Connecticut, 1949. One of the most controversial and inspiring modern residences, architect Johnson's house is composed of two buildings, one with walls entirely of glass, the other of brick. These are carefully related to one another by a garden with sculpture and swimming pool. The brick unit contains a private studio and guest bedrooms. The glass unit is one great room punctuated by a circular fireplace and bathroom, and divided by free-standing storage walls into different living areas. This elegant glass and steel building is a transparent pavilion for viewing the landscaped acres which provide it with privacy and surround it with natural beauty.

168-169   ROME RAILROAD TERMINAL. L. Calini (engineer), E. Montuori, M. Castellazzi, V. Fadigati, A. Pintonello, A. Vitellozzi. Rome, Italy, 1950. Built into a fragment of the ancient Servian wall, this noteworthy station places an advanced structure in a timeless setting. A powerful five-story office building, horizontally organized by long narrow strips of windows, and a light glass and aluminum pavilion for ticket booths and waiting rooms constitute the two major elements. The roof of the pavilion is formed of curved beams cantilevered in front.

170-171   FIRST PRESBYTERIAN CHURCH. Pietro Belluschi. Cottage Grove, Oregon, 1950. The building lot, located in a quiet residential neighborhood, offered Belluschi "wonderful opportunities to create an intimate and inviting atmosphere." The walkway around the courtyard is designed as a transition between the outside world and the sanctuary itself. Attention is strikingly called to the latter by the rising roof line. The plainness of the interior—predominantly light wood and plaster—dramatically counterpointed by a large colored-glass window, makes this church typical of the "Northwest" style of Belluschi.

172-173   UNITED NATIONS SECRETARIAT BUILDING. Wallace K. Harrison, architect in charge. New York, New York, 1950. A slab skyscraper with the inspiration of Le Corbusier, this monumental building is the office of the 3400 employees of the United Nations Secretariat. The ends of the slab are of white marble. The two sides are of green-tinted glass. Atop the tower, an aluminum grille conceals service equipment, and service floors divide the facades into three horizontal parts. Since the axis is north-south, the building has a view of the East River on the east and holds a gigantic mirror to the Manhattan skyline on the west.

174   W. R. HEALY HOUSE. Paul Rudolph and Ralph S. Twitchell. Sarasota, Florida, 1950. The striking feature of this one-story house built on posts is its concave flexible roof. Constructed of steel in tension and covered by a water-tight plastic, it is shallower in the center to allow the rainwater to drain off. The roof lines provide a graceful contrast to the rectangularity of the house itself. The north and south walls are entirely glass. East and west walls are filled with jalousies for solar control.

175   RALPH JOHNSON HOUSE. Harwell H. Harris. Los Angeles, California, 1951. Built into the slope of a hill, this house, a widely admired example of Bay region residential architecture, has three levels. The garage roof serves as a terrace for the living levels. Mr. Harris's exposed frame design, based on a three-foot module, blends into the lush Southern California landscape.

176   MUSEUM OF MODERN ART. Junzo Sakakura. Kamakura, Japan, 1951. This low steel-framed building with walls of asbestos stands on stilts over a water pond and the Japanese landscaping. With the plain windowless facade arranged symmetrically on both sides of a dramatic staircase, the building has a quiet serenity befitting an important museum.

177   UNIVERSITY CITY OF MEXICO LIBRARY. Juan O'Gorman, Gustavo Saavodra, and Juan Martinez de Valesco. Mexico City, Mexico, 1951–1953. This library is one of the most colorful of the famous University City of Mexico buildings and a superb example of the use of the decorative arts in modern architecture. The design of the building is a simple blocklike structure containing bookstacks on a broad one-story base. There are a few small windows, skillfully blended into the large mosaics which are composed of natural stones. The details, almost brutally strong, center around two cosmic wheels reminiscent of the rose windows of the Middle Ages.

178-179   MEMORIAL PEACE CENTER. Kenzo Tange. Hiroshima, Japan, 1951. Nobility and restraint give an added poignancy to this tragic monument. A dramatic parabolic arch provides the background for three low buildings in the large memorial park. In the center is a memorial museum on stilts with louvered, translucent walls. On one side is an assembly hall, on the other an auditorium, both open-frame concrete structures.

180   WEST COLUMBIA ELEMENTARY SCHOOL. Donald Barthelme and Associates. West Columbia, Texas, 1952. A skillful design for a hot climate, this school is freshly aired by an interior landscaped courtyard and has cooling paneled walls. The steel frame in the playground patio is exposed for aesthetic effect. A concrete canopy with undulating roof forms a pleasant and lively contrast to the main rectangular building of the school and shades the driveway.

181   ALCOA BUILDING. Harrison and Abramovitz. Pittsburgh, Pennsylvania, 1952. Appropriately, the building that the Aluminum Corporation of America built for its offices was the first aluminum-sheathed skyscraper in the United States. The walls of this thirty-story tower are made up of prefabricated 6-foot × 12-foot screens of aluminum, each with a window in the center. These windows are reversible. The glass-walled entrance hall, four and a half stories high, has a roof cantilevered from the tower itself.

182-183   LEVER HOUSE. Skidmore, Owings and Merrill; partner in charge: William S. Brown; partner in charge of design: Gordon Bunshaft. New York, New York, 1952. This striking green-glass tower seems to float three stories above the bustle of New York's Park Avenue. The ground floor contains only a lobby and a small service area, leaving almost all the site open for walks and a garden. The second floor, a strip of offices, is raised on columns sheathed in stainless steel. This forms an arcade around the garden. The glistening glass curtain wall mirroring the cityscape about it makes it one of the most influential office buildings in modern architecture.

184-185   CARACAS UNIVERSITY CITY. Carlos Villanueva. Caracas, Venezuela, 1952-1953. One of
the great university cities built recently in South America, Caracas University City
fully exploits the decorative arts for architectural purposes. Leger, Calder, Arp, and Pevsner are
some of the artists. The grandstands of the stadium are covered with vast cantilevered concrete
shells. The Aula Magna, a great auditorium with foyers and a covered plaza, is remarkable acous-
tically, and its ceiling is hung with Calder's huge mobiles under diffused lighting. The play of outside light through the concrete grilles and between the columns of the plaza is especially dramatic.

186   BRATKE HOUSE. Osvaldo Arthur Bratke. São Paulo, Brazil, 1953. A sloping hill, high over
São Paulo, is the setting for Bratke's own home. Designed as a line of rectangles in a
strong slab concrete frame, it is built precisely and with a friendly openness. Brick fillings of varying depth, concrete screens, and glass surfaces give the walls a lively diversity.

187   ROEHAMPTON BUILDING. London County Council. London, England, 1953. A hilly terrain
with old trees is the setting for loosely arranged groups of widely admired apartment
houses for families of varying sizes and incomes. Some eleven-story "maisonette blocks" have grid-
patterned, rectangularly organized fronts, others have dramatically cantilevered balconies. The
terrace and row houses, in contrast, are of English suburban brick design.

188   U. S. EMBASSY HOUSING. Antonin Raymond and L. L. Rado. Tokyo, Japan, 1954. Placed on
a hill and oriented southward for sunlight and breeze are two six-story apartment houses of
reinforced concrete, the first structures of this type in Japan. The main technical problem was protection against earthquakes. The solution was a series of box frames designed to resist shock. The rectangular units of the frame structure are reflected in the exterior. The upper floors contain duplex
apartments, the lower floors efficiency apartments. All have balconies and large glass windows.

189   ELIOT NOYES HOUSE. Eliot Noyes. New Canaan, Connecticut, 1954. This house on a wood-
land site is a worthy example of the modern American residence style. It is, in effect, two
houses under one roof, facing a central patio: one for the adults and formality and the other for
the children and informality. In a direct manner it combines a severely modern plan with natural
New England materials to make a house both tasteful and humane.

190-191   MANUFACTURERS TRUST COMPANY. Skidmore, Owings and Merrill; partner in charge:
William S. Brown; partner in charge of design: Gordon Bunshaft. New York, New
York, 1954. In this four-story glass box, the designers achieved a total departure from the tradi-
tionally solid bank architecture. The entire building is a show window for banking services.
Passers-by can watch the workings of the gleaming vault, which is placed dramatically close to the
street. Open counters replace the traditional tellers' cages, giving an inviting spaciousness to the
interior. Lighting from over-all luminous ceilings gives a crystalline sparkle and brilliance to the
entire building.

192–193   LAMBERT-ST. LOUIS AIRPORT. Yamasaki, Hellmuth and Leinweber. St. Louis, Missouri,
1954. This modern airport is a huge hall roofed by three vast, unpartitioned, concrete
groin vaults which are reminiscent of hangars but designed with much greater complexity. Glass and
aluminum walls, together with these vaults, give an effect of power, smoothness, and transparency.
The low level of the hall serves for plane servicing and freight, the middle level for passenger service.

194-195   MILE HIGH CENTER. I. M. Pei. Denver, Colorado, 1955. The Mile High Center is a towering twenty-one-story rectangular block. The particularly sensitive use of glass in an aluminum and porcelain grid makes both the external and internal structure apparent. Heating and cooling units are visible. The liveliness of the details and the transparency of the whole make an effective contrast to the structural austerity.

196-197   CATFORD SECONDARY SCHOOL. London County Council; J. L. Martin, designer. London, England, 1955. The Catford School was the first school to be designed by the London County Council's own architectural department. The school is designed as two joined blocks: a four-story teaching unit and a single-story assembly hall and gymnasium. The factory-built curtain walls are of glass and lightweight metal. The architects have provided the school with playgrounds which are carefully related to the surrounding wooded parklands by extensive landscaping and planting. Catford School is a worthy example of the justly celebrated British modern school program.

198-200   THE CONNECTICUT GENERAL LIFE INSURANCE COMPANY. Skidmore, Owings and Merrill; partner in charge: William S. Brown; partner in charge of design: Gordon Bunshaft. Bloomfield, Connecticut, 1957. Set in rural beauty on a Connecticut hilltop, this is a building designed to make the fullest possible use of modern office technology. Its huge three-story main building is interrupted only by utility cores and four skillfully designed courtyards. With a cafeteria jutting out over a reflecting pool, an executive wing connected by a covered walkway, and its surrounding landscaped acres, it is a modern complex that may well be a prediction not only of office but of city planning in the future.

Biographies

ALVAR AALTO   Born in 1898 of Finnish-Swedish-Esthonian stock, Aalto was in the forefront of the movement to introduce the new architectural doctrines of the CIAM into Finland following World War I. A graduate of Helsingfors Technical College, he received the opportunity to execute his first independent work, the Industrial Exhibition at Tampere, the year following his graduation. Married to an architect, he is equally famed as a furniture designer and introduced plywood for this purpose. Some of his outstanding works are the Civic Center, Sagnatsalo, Finland; Sunila Factory; Finland; Sanatorium at Paimio, Finland; and the library at Viipuri, Finland.

MAX ABRAMOVITZ   A native of Chicago, Mr. Abramovitz attended the University of Illinois, Columbia University, and École des Beaux Arts in Paris. He is a partner in the firm of Harrison and Abramovitz with offices in New York City. Some of the outstanding works by this firm are the Corning Glass Center, Corning, New York; U. S. Steel Building, Pittsburgh, Pennsylvania; Alcoa Office Building, Pittsburgh, Pennsylvania; and the U. S. Embassy Building, Havana, Cuba.

THE ARCHITECTS' COLLABORATIVE   Formed in 1945, this group of young architects, Jean B. Fletcher, Norman Fletcher, John C. Harkness, Sarah P. Harkness, Robert S. McMillan, Louis A. McMillen, and Benjamin Thompson, joined the celebrated master, Walter Gropius, to execute a series of projects marked by their unusual attention to human values. These are a tribute both to the cooperative spirit of the group and to Gropius' own life long belief in the importance of teamwork in modern architecture.

GUNNAR ASPLUND   The leading Swedish architect of his generation, Asplund, born in Stockholm in 1885, received his architectural training at the Royal Institute of Technology in Stockholm. He later studied under Bergsten, Tengbom, Westman, and Ostberg. He was a teacher, lecturer, and world traveler. Some of his more recognized works include Stockholm City Library; Stockholm Exposition; State Bacteriological Laboratory, Stockholm; and, the last of his completed works, the Crematorium at Skogskyrkogarden, Stockholm. He died in 1940.

DONALD BARTHELME   This native Texan received his education at Rice Institute and the University of Pennsylvania. A gifted architect, he is perhaps best known for his excellent schools. His present firm, Donald Barthelme and Associates, was organized in 1939. Mr. Barthelme has received many honors for his distinctive contribution to the advancement of our schools through better design. Some of his award-winning schools are St. Rose of Lima, Houston, Texas; West Columbia Elementary School, West Columbia, Texas; Sweeny Elementary School, Sweeny, Texas.

PIETRO BELLUSCHI   Pietro Belluschi was born in Ancona, Italy, on August 18, 1899. He attended the University of Rome and received a degree in civil engineering at Cornell University. After working in the office of A. E. Doyle in Portland as chief designer from 1927–1943, he set up his own office as design consultant, particularly for churches, offices, and shopping centers. His "Northwest Architecture," developed with an eye to the Japanese vernacular, with extensive use of regional woods, has become internationally renowned. As head of the Department of Architecture at the Massachusetts Institute of Technology in Cambridge, Massachusetts, he has been an important influence in education and his profession. Among his outstanding buildings are the Portland Art Museum; the Equitable Savings and Loan Association, Portland, Oregon; and the First Presbyterian Church, Cottage Grove, Oregon.

OSVALDO ARTHUR BRATKE   A native of Brazil, Bratke was born in 1907 in São Paulo and studied at Universidade MacKenzie there. He maintains his architectural office in São Paulo. The home he designed for himself is recognized as one of the most striking examples of South American architecture to be found today.

MARCEL BREUER   Born in 1902 in the town of Pecs in southern Hungary, Breuer's earliest ambition was to become a painter or sculptor. He joined the Bauhaus in Weimar founded by Walter Gropius. His creation of tubular steel furniture was one of the most important influences on modern furniture design. In 1937, with Walter Gropius, he came to the United States and Harvard University. A few of his more notable works include Breuer House (with Gropius), Lincoln, Massachusetts; Chamberlain House (with Gropius), Sudbury, Massachusetts; Dolderthal Apartments (with Alfred Roth), Zurich, Switzerland; Robinson House, Williamstown, Massachusetts; and Breuer House, New Canaan, Connecticut. He lives in New Canaan, Connecticut, and has offices in New York City.

J. A. BRINKMAN   Born in 1902 in Rotterdam, Brinkman received his technical training at Technischen Hochschule in Delft. In 1925 he joined with L. C. van der Vlugt, with whom he designed the famous van Nelle factory in Rotterdam. After van der Vlugt's death, he associated with J. H. van der Broek. He is an active member of BNA (Associated Netherland Architects).

GORDON BUNSHAFT   Born in Buffalo, New York, and educated at Massachusetts Institute of Technology, Gordon Bunshaft has received world-wide recognition as partner in charge of design with the architectural firm of Skidmore, Owings and Merrill. He joined this organization in 1945 after serving with the Corps of Engineers in the U. S. Army. His office and home are in New York City. Some of Bunshaft's more outstanding works with Skidmore, Owings and Merrill are Lever House, New York City; Manufacturers Trust Company Bank, New York City; U. S. Air Force Academy, Colorado Springs, Colorado; H. J. Heinz Company, Pittsburgh, Pennsylvania; and Connecticut General Life Insurance Office Building, Bloomfield, Connecticut.

LEO CALINI   Calini was born in Ancona, Italy, in 1903. In 1927 he received a degree in civil engineering at Rome. He specializes in hospitals and schools. Mr. Calini's associate is the architect E. Montuori.

MASSIMO CASTELLAZZI   Castellazzi was born in Ancona, Italy, in 1901. At Rome in 1926 he received a degree in architecture. He is recognized for his work in public and commercial buildings. Castellazzi's partners are V. Fadigati, A. Pintonello, and A. Vitellozzi.

LUCIO COSTA   Lucio Costa is one of the leaders of modern architecture in South America. He was born in Toulon, France, in 1902. He studied in England and France and at Escola Nacional de Belas Artes, Rio de Janeiro. Working alone or with other architects, he has designed excellent apartment houses and civic and government buildings that have brought international recognition to Brazil. In 1936, Costa worked with Le Corbusier and other Brazilian architects on the new Ministry of Education and Public Health. In 1939, Costa and Niemeyer were chosen to erect a pavilion embodying the new principles of Brazilian architecture at the New York World's Fair. Among Costa's other works are his apartment houses in Rio de Janeiro and his house for Argemero Hungria Machado.

WILLIAM DUDOK   Born in Amsterdam in 1884, this architect, engineer, and town planner received his education at the Royal Military Academy at Breda and remained in the army until 1913. As town architect for Hilversum, he built its famed town hall. As a town planner he created extension and reconstruction schemes at Hilversum, The Hague, Velsen, Wassevaar, and Zwalle. Other works of this internationally honored architect include the Crematory at Westerveld; Netherlands Students' House of the Cité Universitaire, Paris; "De Bijenkorf," Rotterdam; and the office building for the Royal Dutch Steelworks, Velsen.

CHARLES EAMES   A noted designer as well as an architect, Charles Eames was born in St. Louis, Missouri, in 1907. Eames studied architecture at Washington University and in 1938, after six years of architectural practice in St. Louis, he won a fellowship at the Cranbrook Academy of Art. At Cranbrook he worked with Eliel and Eero Saarinen, helping to develop the Experimental Design Department. In 1940, with Eero Saarinen, he won first prizes in the Organic Design Competition conducted by the Museum of Modern Art. One of these was for his now famous chair of

moulded plywood. In the field of architecture, Eames is best known for his own house near Los Angeles, California, skillfully designed of standard building components.

VASCO FADIGATI   Born in Trieste in 1902, Fadigati received a degree in architecture at Venice in 1928. He is known for his work on the Rome Railroad Terminal. Fadigati's architectural partners are M. Castellazzi, A. Pintonello, and A. Vitellozzi.

LUIGI FIGINI   Born in Milan in 1903, Luigi Figini received in 1926 at Milan a degree in architecture. He is a founder of the group called "7," the MIAR, and the magazine *Quadrante*. He is also a member of the International Congress for Modern Architecture (CIAM), an organization founded by architects in Switzerland in 1928 to discuss the techniques and developments of modern architecture. Figini is also a noted author and interior designer.

WALTER GROPIUS   One of the most influential international architectural figures of this era, Walter Gropius was born in 1883 in Berlin, Germany. He received his education there and worked with the famed Peter Behrens. In 1918 Gropius founded the Bauhaus which became the virtual preparatory school for the modern international style. He remained in Dessau with the school and designed its famed glass and steel building. He came to America, after an interval in England, and in 1938 became chairman of the Harvard Architectural Department. In 1946 he returned to active architectural practice as a member of The Architects' Collaborative, in keeping with his convictions concerning group design. His pioneering works—Fagus Shoe Company factory, Alfeld, Germany; and Bauhaus School and City Employment Office, both in Dessau, Germany—are only one measure of a man who is not only a master architect but a master educator.

HARWELL H. HARRIS   Harwell Harris was born in Redlands, California, in 1903. A graduate of California's Pomona College, he has lectured as a visiting critic at Columbia and Yale Universities and was head of the School of Architecture at the University of Texas from 1951–1955. Harris is best known as one of the Pacific Coast's most outstanding residential architects, combining an understanding of modern construction with an appreciation of the way people live. Outstanding examples of his work are the Havens House in Berkeley and the Johnson House in Los Angeles.

WALLACE K. HARRISON   Wallace K. Harrison was born in 1895 in Worcester, Massachusetts. He left school at 14 and later took a course in construction engineering at Worcester Tech. At 20 he went to New York and began work for McKim, Mead and White. In the 1930's, he was recognized for his work with the team of architects designing Rockefeller Center and his theme building for the New York World's Fair. Harrison was the planning director of the United Nations Secretariat Building, and, more recently, for the Alcoa Building, Pittsburgh, Pennsylvania, and the Corning Glass Center in Corning, New York. His present firm is Harrison and Abramovitz.

GEORGE HELLMUTH   George Hellmuth was born in St. Louis, Missouri, in 1907. He received his B.A. and his architectural degree from Washington University. The university awarded him a Steedman Fellowship, enabling him to study in Europe. From 1949–1954 he was a member of the firm of Hellmuth, Yamasaki and Leinweber.

During these years his outstanding works were apartment buildings in St. Louis and the renowned Lambert—St. Louis Airport Terminal. In 1954, the present firm, Hellmuth, Obata and Kassabaum, was organized.

RAYMOND M. HOOD   Born in Pawtucket, Rhode Island, in 1881, Hood was educated at Massachusetts Institute of Technology and École des Beaux Arts. In association with John Mead Howells he won the international competition for the Chicago Tribune Tower. He served as consultant on the rebuilding of the University of Brussels and was the associate architect for the Century of Progress Fair, Chicago, 1933. The Daily News Building, New York City, by Hood and Howells, is ranked as one of the world's outstanding buildings. Other notable works are the Beaux Arts Apartments and the McGraw-Hill Building, both in New York City. Hood's work with the group of architects planning Rockefeller Center was the climactic contribution of an architect who built skyscrapers. He died in 1934.

SUTEMI HORIGUCHI   Born in 1895 and graduated from Tokyo University, Horiguchi is an internationally famous architect and author. An outstanding authority on buildings for the tea ceremony, he is a member of the Japanese Institute of Architects and has his office in Tokyo. Among Horiguchi's principal works are his Okada House and Gardens, Tokyo, and his Wakasa House, Tokyo.

GEORGE HOWE   George Howe was born in Worcester, Massachusetts, in 1886 and as a child traveled throughout Europe. He attended school in Switzerland and New England and in 1904 went to Harvard, where he was influenced by Charles Moore. In 1907 he went to École des Beaux Arts in Paris. Returning to the United States, he founded a partnership with Mellor and Meigs in Philadelphia and in 1929 he joined with William Lescaze to form the famed partnership of Howe and Lescaze. From 1950–1954 Howe was a distinguished chairman of the Department of Architecture at Yale University. Howe died in 1955.

JOHN MEAD HOWELLS   The son of William Dean Howells, John Mead Howells was born in 1868 in Cambridge, Massachusetts. He received his education at Massachusetts Institute of Technology, Harvard, and École des Beaux Arts, Paris. In 1922, he was sent to Belgium by President Hoover's relief organization as commissioner to lay out plans for the University of Brussels. Besides the Daily News Building in New York City, his works include the Title Guarantee and Trust Building and the Chicago Tribune Tower.

ARNE JACOBSEN   Arne Jacobsen was born in 1902 in Copenhagen. His earliest interests were sports and art and it was at the urging of his father that he studied architecture. He received his training at the Copenhagen Technical College and in 1927 he graduated from the Danish Royal Academy. His Bella Vista Flats of the early 1930's are still among the finest apartments in Europe while other outstanding buildings are his town halls at Aarhus and at Rodovre near Copenhagen. A meticulous workman with a keen sense of design in the modern Danish tradition, he has also gained recognition for his silverware, lighting fixtures, and furniture.

PIERRE JEANNERET   Born in Geneva in 1896, Pierre Jeanneret studied at École des Beaux Arts in Geneva. A painter and furniture designer as well as an architect, he went to Paris in 1920 and worked for two years with August Perret. In 1922 he joined his cousin, Le Corbusier, and has collaborated with him on many projects. Among

these are the Villa Savoye, Poissy-sur-Seine, and the Cité Universitaire, Paris.

PHILIP JOHNSON   Philip Johnson is the unique example of a celebrated architectural critic who became an equally celebrated architect. Born in Cleveland, Ohio, in 1906 he did his undergraduate and graduate work at Harvard University. As an author, lecturer, and for over 20 years as director of the Department of Architecture at the Museum of Modern Art in New York City, Johnson has brought the modern movement to the attention of the public. His work —such as his own glass house in New Canaan, Connecticut; the Hodgson House in New Canaan, Connecticut; the KTI Synagogue in Port Chester, New York, and in collaboration with Mies van der Rohe on the Seagram's building in New York City—has brought him recognition as a leading American architect.

ALBERT KAHN   Albert Kahn was brought to this country by his parents as a child. He began his architectural career as an office boy to an architect. At the age of 34, with 22 years of experience behind him in architectural firms, he was asked to design his first factory. This job for Packard Motor Company was the first reinforced concrete factory in America. He has specialized in factory design and today the effects of the industrial design talent of Albert Kahn can be seen all over the world. Outstanding examples of Kahn's work in the American factory style are the De Soto Press Shop, Detroit, Michigan; the Engineering Laboratory of the Ford Motor Company, Dearborn, Michigan; and the Dodge Truck Plant, Detroit, Michigan.

LE CORBUSIER   Charles Édouard Jeanneret, known by his architectural pseudonym, Le Corbusier, was born on October 6, 1887, in Le Chaux-de-Fonds, Switzerland. In 1908, Le Corbusier became an apprentice to Perret, a pioneer in ferroconcrete construction. After two years, he went to Berlin to enter the workshop of Peter Behrens, working there with Mies van der Rohe and Walter Gropius. It was with another architect, Ozenfant, that he founded the revolutionary design review *Espirit nouveau*, after World War I. In 1921 he began an architectural partnership with his cousin Pierre Jeanneret, and in 1923 his book, *Towards a New Architecture,* explained the architectural theories expressed in his buildings. Famed for his inventive and aesthetic approach to architecture, his important theories and great works have made him one of the most influential geniuses of our time. Among Le Corbusier's masterpieces are Villa Savoye, Poissy-sur-Seine; Swiss pavilion at the Cité Universitaire, Paris; Chapel at Ronchamp, France, and Chandigarh, the new city in India.

JOSEPH A. LEINWEBER   Leinweber was born in Wheeling, West Virginia, in 1895 and received his education at Carnegie Institute of Technology. He was a member of our early Army Air Corps during World War I. He now makes his home in Detroit, Michigan, where he is a partner in the firm of Yamasaki and Leinweber. Some of their better-known works are the U. S. Army Research and Development Center, Detroit; Lambert-St. Louis Airport Terminal Building, St. Louis; U. S. Army Personnel Records Center, St. Louis.

WILLIAM LESCAZE   A native of Geneva, Switzerland, Lescaze gained architectural recognition in the United States. He has received numerous awards and honors for such works as the famed Philadelphia Savings Fund Society Building, Philadelphia; CBS California Headquarters, Hollywood, California; and Williamsburg Houses,

Brooklyn, New York City. He is a lecturer and critic at many leading architectural schools.

LONDON COUNTY COUNCIL   Founded in 1888 as the central administrative body for the metropolis of London, the London County Council delegates the administration of its policy to 15 departments, one of which is its Architectural Department. Because of the need for a central coordination of the enormous amount of building after the war, the County of London Plan was prepared in 1943 to outline a building program for Greater London as well as to administer the planning, zoning, and building codes for all architectural developments. Through this plan, the department has concentrated its work on community buildings: schools, civic centers, and churches.

ROBERT MAILLART   Robert Maillart, one of the great shape-givers of modern architecture, was born in Bern, Switzerland, and received his degree in structural engineering at the Federal Institute of Technology in Zurich in 1894. He is renowned for a series of reinforced concrete bridges generally considered some of the twentieth century's most beautiful structures. In 1936 Maillart was elected an honorary member of the Royal Institute of British Architects. He died in Geneva in 1940. Among Maillart's best-known works are the Bridge over the River Arve, near Geneva; the Salginatobel Bridge; the Bridge over the River Thur; and the Schwandbach Bridge.

ERIC MENDELSOHN   Born in 1887 in the town of Allanstein in East Prussia, Mendelsohn's young life was spent in the shadows of a Gothic church and a castle built by German knights who conquered the country. He studied architecture at Berlin Technische Hochschule and later at a school by the same name in Munich. His first important work was the Einstein Tower in Potsdam, 1920. Then came the Berliner Tageblatt Building with Neutra in 1923. He has been called the representative architect of the age of industrialization and the machine. Mendelsohn died in 1953, leaving many notable works. Among them are the German Metal Workers' Union Building, Berlin; Schocken Department Store, Chemnitz, Germany; and the Temple and Community Center, St. Paul, Minnesota.

LUDWIG MIES VAN DER ROHE   No master architect has been more aware of this age of science and technology than Mies van der Rohe and none has designed more magnificently in terms of it. Born in 1886, in Aachen, Germany, he learned building, without academic training, by working from a stone mason's assistant to Peter Behrens' apprentice. A recognized leader of modern architectural thought in post-World-War-I Germany, it was his superb German Pavilion for the International Exhibition at Barcelona, Spain, in 1929 and the Tugendhat House in Brno, Czechoslovakia, in 1930 that brought recognition throughout the world. In 1930, he left the directorship of the Bauhaus in a Germany officially growing anti-modern to accept the directorship of architecture at what is now the Illinois Institute of Technology. His buildings for its new campus, as well as his famed Lakeshore Drive Apartments in Chicago, Illinois, and the Seagram's building in New York City, are masterpieces of a great master.

EUGENIO MONTUORI   Born in 1907 in Pesaro, Montuori received a degree in architecture at Rome in 1931. He is an assistant professor of city planning at the Polytechnic Institute at Rome and also has prepared exhibitions of interior design. One of the best-known architects of post-war Italy, he is renowned for city planning, churches and public buildings such as the Rome Railroad Terminal.

JORGE MACHADO MOREIRA   Born in Paris in 1904, Jorge Machado Moreira, a Brazilian, was educated at Escola Nacional de Belas Artes in Rio de Janeiro. He is best known for his work on the Ministry of Education and Public Health, Rio de Janeiro, and the design of the Institute for Child Welfare at the University of Brazil, Rio de Janeiro.

PIER LUIGI NERVI   Nervi, one of the great structural engineers of our time, was born in Sondrio in 1891 and received an engineering degree at Bologna in 1931. He holds a professorship in Technology and Construction Techniques at the University of Rome and is a member of the CIAM. A modern master of prestressed concrete, his widely influential works are the airplane hangers of Buenos Aires, the Tobacco Warehouse at Bologna, the Salt Warehouse in Tortona, the Turin Exhibition Halls, and the Olympic Sports Palace in Rome. Through his theory and example he has added shell structures to the vocabulary of modern architecture.

RICHARD J. NEUTRA   One of the most highly respected designers in the modern idiom, Richard Neutra was born in Vienna on April 8, 1892, and studied at the universities of Vienna and Zurich. After some years of work in Switzerland, he came to the United States where most of his work has been executed, although Neutra has interested himself in the architectural problems of Latin America and has worked in a number of these countries. Among his well-known California houses are the Lovell House, Los Angeles, and the Desert House, Palm Springs. The Experimental School, Los Angeles, and the Channel Heights Housing Project, San Pedro, are other examples of Neutra's distinctive architecture. His extensive writings are a significant contribution to architectural literature.

OSCAR NIEMEYER   The Brazilian architect, Oscar Niemeyer, was born in 1907. After his formal education at Barabitas College, he received an architectural degree from Escola Nacional de Belas Artes, Rio de Janeiro, in 1934. He joined the office of Lucio Costa for several years. Niemeyer first won recognition in 1936 when he was invited to participate in the famous Ministry of Education and Public Health project on which Le Corbusier was the consultant. Niemeyer works closely with sculptors and painters and has incorporated many of their works into his architecture. His Brazilian buildings are known for plasticity and dramatic uses of space. Among Niemeyer's important works are his Boavista Bank, Rio de Janeiro; Church of St. Francis, Pampulha; and his own house in Rio de Janeiro.

ELIOT NOYES   Noted as an industrial designer as well as an architect, Noyes was born in 1910 in Boston and received his education at Harvard University. In 1935–1936 he served as architect on an Iranian archaeological expedition. For several years he was director of the Department of Industrial Design at the Museum of Modern Art, New York City. His present firm is Eliot Noyes and Associates, New Canaan, Connecticut. Architecturally, Noyes is perhaps best known for his residential work, especially for his concrete "bubble houses" at Hobe Sound and his own award-winning home in New Canaan.

JUAN O'GORMAN   An early exponent of modern architecture in Mexico, Juan O'Gorman is of Irish descent and has long been interested in the integration of Indian and Christian cultures. He is a painter and has done many mosaics, a medium popular in Mexico. With Gustavo Saavedra and Juan Martinez de Velasco, he designed the celebrated central library for the government-sponsored University City of Mexico.

J. J. P. OUD   J. J. P. Oud, one of the most influential pioneers of the modern architectural movement, was born in Purmerend, Holland, in 1890. He was educated at Quellinus Arts and Crafts School, and at Rijksnormaalschool, both in Amsterdam. In 1910–1911 he studied at the Technical School of the University of Delft, where he met H. P. Berlage. In 1917 he founded the review and group de Stijl with the painters Mondrian, von Doesburg, Vantongerloo, and van der Leck. He was appointed, soon afterwards, architect in charge of city housing in Rotterdam. Among Oud's best-known works are the workers' houses at the Hook of Holland and the Shell Building at The Hague.

I. M. PEI   I. M. Pei was born in Canton, China, and decided to become an architect after seeing his first skyscraper under construction in Shanghai at the age of 16. He went to Massachusetts Institute of Technology in 1935 and later to the Harvard Graduate School of Design. Working in collaboration with William Zeckendorf of Webb and Knapp, real estate developers, he designed Mile High Center in Denver, Colorado, and Roosevelt Field Shopping Center on Long Island. His firm, I. M. Pei and Associates, is located in New York City and for the most part concentrates its considerable talent on commercial buildings and urban redevelopment projects.

ACHILLE PINTONELLO   Born in Pianiga, Venice, in 1902, Pintonello received a civil engineering degree with a specialty in architecture at Padua in 1925. In 1927–1928 he was an assistant in architecture on the faculty of engineering at Padua. He has done civil buildings, industrial and commercial buildings, schools, churches, and hospitals. Pintonello's architectural associates are M. Castellazzi, V. Fadigati, and A. Vitellozzi.

GINO POLLINI   Born in Rovereto, Trento, in 1903, Gino Pollini received a degree in architecture at Milan in 1927. He is one of the founders of the group called "7," of the MIAR, and the magazine, Quadrante. He is Italian delegate to the CIAM and has had exhibitions of interior design for homes and shops and civil buildings.

L. L. RADO   A resident of Czechoslovakia until 1939, Rado came to the United States and worked in Boston until 1943. In 1944 he formed, with Antonin Raymond, the architectural firm of Antonin Raymond and L. L. Rado with offices in New York City and Tokyo. Rado received his architectural training at Technical University in Prague and Harvard University. His bold use of modern materials can be seen in works like The Electrolux Industrial Buildings and Recreational Center, Old Greenwich, Connecticut; Reader's Digest Building, Tokyo; and apartment buildings for the U. S. Embassy, Tokyo.

ANTONIN RAYMOND   Born in Kladno, Bohemia, Austria, and educated at the Polytechnic Institute in Prague, Czechoslovakia, Raymond makes his home in New Hope, Pennsylvania. His present firm, Antonin Raymond and L. L. Rado, has offices in New York City and Tokyo. Raymond has successfully combined the techniques of modern European architecture with the Japanese spirit and tradition. Some of the outstanding examples of his work in Japan are St. Luke's Medical Center, Tokyo; U. S. Embassy, Tokyo; and Reader's Digest Building, Tokyo. He is a world traveler and has been honored by many nations for his contributions to architecture and society.

AFFONSO EDUARDO REIDY   Affonso Eduardo Reidy, born in Paris, 1909, is one of South America's notable architects. He was educated in Rio de Janeiro at Escola Nacional de Belas Artes and has his office in that city. His most famous works are his Museum of Modern Art, Rio de Janeiro, his "Pedregulho" housing development, Rio de Janeiro, and his contribution to the design of the Ministry of Education and Public Health, Rio de Janeiro.

MARCEL AND MILTON ROBERTO   Marcel and Milton Roberto, young Brazilian architects educated in Rio de Janeiro, have worked together since they won a competition for the Brazilian Press Association Building. A third brother, Mauricio, joined them in 1941. International recognition has been given to their South American buildings. Marcel and Mauricio have recently been commissioned to develop a large tourist center in Algiers. Milton was killed in an automobile accident in 1953.

ALFRED ROTH   Born in 1903 near Bern, Switzerland, Alfred Roth's earliest interest was painting. In 1926 he received his diploma from ETH in Zurich and went to work in the office of Karl Moser. After working in various architectural offices he opened an independent office in 1932. His works include private houses, factories, and military buildings. A writer, designer, architect, and editor of Werk Magazine, he is a member of many professional architectural and design organizations.

PAUL RUDOLPH   Born in Kentucky, Paul Rudolph received his architectural training at Alabama Polytechnic Institute and Harvard University. Outstanding examples of Rudolph's imaginative buildings are the Sanderling Beach Cabana Club, The Umbrella House, and the Healy House, all in Sarasota, Florida. He has received many honors and awards as an outstanding younger architect and is chairman of the Department of Architecture at Yale University.

EERO SAARINEN   Second-generation talents usually have a hard time gaining recognition. It is typical of Eero Saarinen that he is an exception, even though he preferred to work in his famous father's shadow. He was born in Finland on August 20, 1910, and studied sculpture in Paris and architecture at Yale University. He has his home and office in Bloomfield Hills, Michigan, near the Cranbrook Academy designed by his father. He worked with his father on projects ranging from the Crow Island School, Winnetka, Illinois, to the Opera Shed at the Berkshire Music Center in Massachusetts. His own work, from the auditorium and chapel at Massachusetts Institute of Technology in Cambridge, Massachusetts, to the vast General Motors Technical Center, outside Detroit, Michigan, has established the young Saarinen as one of the most respected and talented architects of his generation.

ELIEL SAARINEN   Eliel Saarinen, one of the great architects and planners of his time, was born in 1873 in Rantasalmi, Finland. He received his education in Finland and traveled extensively, making lasting friendships with such famed cultural leaders as Mahler, Gorki, Sibelius, Maroti, and Milles. Saarinen came to the United States in 1923 with his family. He designed and headed the Cranbrook Academy of Art at Bloomfield Hills, Michigan, receiving honors from every corner of the world for his contribution to architecture. Eliel Saarinen died in 1950. With his son, Eero, he designed the Summer Opera House at the Berkshire Music Center, Lenox, Massachusetts; Tabernacle Church of Christ, Columbus, Indiana; and the celebrated Crow Island School, Winnetka, Illinois.

JUNZO SAKAKURA   Junzo Sakakura was born in 1904 and received his education at Tokyo University. He worked with Le Corbusier from 1931 to 1936 in his architectural atelier in Paris. An outstanding member of the Japan Institute of Architects as well as CIAM, he works through the J. Sakakura Architectural Institute in Tokyo. Among Sakakura's important works are his Japanese Pavilion at the 1937 Paris Exposition and his Museum of Modern Art in Kamakura, near Tokyo, 1951.

SKIDMORE, OWINGS AND MERRILL   Founded in 1936 by Louis Skidmore and Nathaniel A. Owings, this outstanding architectural organization adopted its present name three years later when joined by John O. Merrill. Today with other partners, and participating associates in New York, Chicago, Portland, and San Francisco, this firm has become renowned for large-scale projects executed with distinguished skill, precision, and imagination. Typical are the celebrated Manufacturers Trust Company and Lever House in New York City, Connecticut General Life Insurance Company in Bloomfield, Connecticut, and government buildings at Oak Ridge, Tennessee.

KENZO TANGE   The Japanese architect, Kenzo Tange, was born in 1913. He graduated from Tokyo University where he is now a professor. Besides the Memorial Peace Center in Hiroshima, his works include his own home, Tsuda College Library, Tokyo, a printing plant at Nara, and a city hall in Shinji.

THE TECTON GROUP   In 1932, the midst of the depression, seven British architects, feeling that working cooperatively would be more successful, pioneered the idea of group architecture in England. The Tecton Group was commissioned to construct the Penguin Pool, one of a series of imaginative buildings they did for the Regent's Park Zoo in London. In 1934, they designed a series of small houses in Sussex and in 1935 the renowned apartments at Highgate. The partnership was dissolved in 1949. Three of the group, Skinner, Drake and Lasdun, have since formed a new firm.

GIUSEPPE TERRAGNI   Giuseppe Terragni was born in Milan in 1904. He graduated in 1926 from the Polytechnic Institute of Milan and was one of the influential group "7" who wrote articles on architecture. Besides the Casa del Popolo, his works include Casa del Fascio, Asilo Infantile, and numerous projects for competitions.

EDUARDO TORROJA   This Spanish engineer is famous for his pioneer work in prefabricated concrete forms and is a director of the Institute of Cement Construction. Two widely influential books by him are *Elasticity; with application to construction technology* and *Method for Calculating Prestressed Reinforced Concrete*. Among Torroja's principal works are the L'Instituto Construzioni e Cementi and his Hippodrome, both in Madrid.

RALPH S. TWITCHELL   Born in 1891, Ralph Twitchell was educated at Rollins, McGill, and Columbia Universities, receiving degrees in arts, architecture, and structural engineering. He became associated with the architect Paul Rudolph in 1940, and he lives in Sarasota, Florida. Two of his well-known residences designed in partnership with Paul Rudolph are the W. R. Healy House and the Miller House, both in Sarasota, Florida.

L. C. VAN DER VLUGT   Born in 1896 in Rotterdam, van der Vlugt received his architectural training as an apprentice working in various architectural offices. One of the distinguished architects of Europe, he formed a partnership in 1925 with J. A. Brinkman that lasted until his death in 1936. Some of van der Vlugt's principal works, done in association with Brinkman, are the Van Nelle Factory, the Bergpolder Flats, Rotterdam, and the Sonneveid House, Rotterdam.

CARLOS RAUL VILLANUEVA   Carlos Raul Villanueva, a leading South American architect, was born in Croydon, England, in 1900 and studied at École des Beaux Arts in Paris. Villaneuva became well-known in Latin America through his architectural work at University City, in Caracas. Among his most noted achievements there are the Olympic Stadium and the Aula Magna (auditorium) with its covered plaza. He lives in Caracas, Venezuela, where he is a professor at the university.

ANNIBALE VITELLOZZI   Born in Anghiari, Arezzo, in 1902, Annibale Vitellozzi received a degree in architecture at Rome in 1927. He is well known for transportation and civic buildings. Vitellozzi's architectural associates are M. Castellazzi, V. Fadigati, and A. Pintonello.

FRANK LLOYD WRIGHT   The most famous architect America has produced is also a noted public figure. He has brought modern architectural design to the attention of the public. This is perhaps natural for a man whose father was a preacher and mother a teacher, but what was not expected in midwestern America was a genius who would change the course of architecture. Frank Lloyd Wright was born in Wisconsin in 1869, studied engineering at that state's university and worked in Chicago with the master Louis Sullivan. His works, from houses like the Robie House, Chicago, Illinois; the Avery Coonley House, Riverside, Illinois; the Rose Pauson House, Phoenix, Arizona; and the famous "Falling Waters" in Bear Run, Pennsylvania; to buildings like Unity Temple, Oak Park, Illinois; Taliesin West, Arizona; and the Price Tower, Bartlesville, Oklahoma, show a natural range and imagination unexcelled in modern architecture.

MINORU YAMASAKI   Born in Seattle, Washington, Minoru Yamasaki was educated at the University of Washington and New York University and has traveled extensively throughout the world. He worked as a designer with several leading firms before joining the architectural partnership, Hellmuth, Yamasaki and Leinweber. In the many projects of his present firm, Yamasaki and Leinweber, with offices in Detroit, Michigan, he demonstrates the imagination and style which mark him as one of the most promising American architects of his generation.

PHOTOGRAPHIC CREDITS

Courtesy Alcoa: p. 181 (2)

Courtesy American-Swedish News Exchange: pp. 142, 143 (2)

Wayne Andrews: pp. 20 (top), 24 (bottom)

Courtesy The Architects' Collaborative: pp. 126, 127 (top) by Robert Damora; p. 127 (bottom) by Fred Stone

Architectural Journal: pp. 196 (2), 197

Architectural Review: pp. 153, 187 (2)

Charles T. Branford: p. 92

Courtesy Marcel Breuer: p. 99 (bottom); pp. 120, 121 (3) by Robert Damora

P. Cartoni: pp. 168, 169

Chicago Architectural Photographing Co.: pp. 42, 43

Courtesy Danish National Tourist Office: p. 157

Fred R. Dapprich: p. 175 (2)

Courtesy French Embassy, Information Division: p. 15

Ewing Galloway: p. 16 (top) by Burton Holmes

Maurey Garber: p. 90 (2)

Marcel Gautherot: pp. 116 (2), 117, 130

Philip Gendreau: p. 16 (bottom) by G. A. Douglas; pp. 18, 144, 149, 172

Courtesy General Motors Corporation: p. 128

Courtesy Walter Gropius: pp. 91, 93

P. E. Guerrero: pp. 58 (2), 59

Courtesy Consulate General of Japan: pp. 151, 176, 178, 179

Courtesy S. C. Johnson and Son Inc.: pp. 52, 53

From *Space, Time and Architecture: The Growth of a New Tradition*, Sigfried Giedion, Harvard University Press, Cambridge, Mass., 1941, 1949, 1954: pp. 17 (2), 22, 91

Hedrich-Blessing: pp. 84 (top), 89, by Hube Henry; pp. 50 (2), 51, 86 (2), 87 (2), 192 (2), 193 (bottom), by Bill Hedrich; pp. 20 (bottom), 41, 44, 84 (bottom), 85 (top), by Bill Engdahl; pp. 82, 83, 85 (bottom and center), 111 (2), 154, 155, 158 (2), 159

Lucien Hervé: pp. 62 (2), 63 (2), 64 (2), 65 (2), 70 (3), 72 (2), 73 (3), 75 (top), 76

From *Sixty Years of Living Architecture*, Frank Lloyd Wright, Horizon Press, New York: p. 49

F. S. Lincoln: p. 156 (2)

Rollie McKenna: pp. 161, 162, 163, 177 (2), 184 (2), 185 (2), 186

Ulric Meisel: p. 180 (2)

Courtesy Mrs. Eric Mendelsohn: pp. 139 (2), 141 (3)

Courtesy Olivetti: p. 152

Courtesy Netherlands Information Service: p. 137 (2)

Courtesy Netherlands National Tourist Office: p. 140

Courtesy Richard J. Neutra: pp. 94, 95 (top), by Luckhaus Studio

Courtesy William Lescaze: p. 145 (2)

Courtesy H. C. Price Co.: pp. 60, 61

Courtesy Raymond and Rado: p. 188 (3)

From *Oscar Niemeyer: Works in Progress*, edited by Stamo Papadaki, Reinhold Publishing Corp., New York: p. 131 (3)

Courtesy Rockefeller Center Inc.: p. 148 by Impact Photo Inc.

From *Adolph Loos*, H. Kulka, Schröll, Vienna, 1931: p. 25 (top)

Julius Shulman: pp. 25 (bottom), 54 (2), 55, 56 (bottom), 57, 95 (bottom), 100 (2), 101, 118 (2), 119 (2), 122, 123, 164, 165 (3), 170, 171 (2), 194, 195 (2)

Ernst Sheidegger: pp. 74 (2), 75 (bottom), 77

Courtesy Skidmore, Owings and Merrill: p. 182, by J. A. Langley

G. E. Kidder Smith: pp. 26, 66, 68 (2), 69, 99, 102, 103, 106 (2), 107, 108 (2), 109, 110, 112, 113, 124, 125, 138, 150

Courtesy Spanish State Tourist Office: p. 24 (top)

Ezra Stoller: pp. 46 (2), 47, 56 (top), 88, 114 (2), 115, 129 (2), 132 (2), 133, 166, 167, 173, 174 (2), 183, 189 (2), 190, 191 (2), 193 (top), 198 (2), 199, 200

Courtesy Swiss National Tourist Office: pp. 96, 97, 98, 104

Thomas Airviews: p. 146

Courtesy Time: p. 136 (2), by David Lees

Courtesy E. J. Torroja: pp. 134 (2), 135

Wide World Photos: p. 147

BIBLIOGRAPHY

The following sources were found to be particularly helpful in preparing this volume:

Books:

American Guide Series, New York City Guide, Random House, New York, 1939.

Amsterdam, G. van Saane, and Krovnder, F. G., *Willem M. Dudok,* Bussum, 1954

Andrews, Wayne, *Architecture, Ambition and Americans,* Harper & Brothers, New York, 1955.

Barr, A. H., Jr., and Hitchcock, H. R. (and others), *Modern Architects,* Museum of Modern Art, New York, 1932.

Barr, A. H., Jr., Hitchcock, H. R., Jr., Mumford, L., and Johnson, P., *Modern Architecture International Exhibition,* Museum of Modern Art, New York, 1932.

Bill, Max, *Robert Maillart,* H. Girsberger, Zurich, 1955.

Blake, Peter, *Marcel Breuer: Architect and Designer,* F. W. Dodge, New York, 1949.

Blake, Peter, *Marcel Breuer: Sun & Shadow,* Dodd Mead & Company, New York, 1956.

Breines, S., and Kocher, A. L., *Architecture & Furniture,* Aalto, Museum of Modern Art, New York, 1938.

Cheney, Sheldon, *The New World Architecture,* Longmans, New York, 1930.

Christ-Janer, *Eliel Saarinen,* University of Chicago Press, 1948.

Drexler, Arthur, *The Architecture of Japan,* Museum of Modern Art, New York, 1955.

Giedion, Sigfried, *Space, Time and Architecture: The Growth of a New Tradition,* Harvard University Press, Cambridge, 1954.

Giedion, Sigfried, *Walter Gropius, Work and Teamwork,* Reinhold Publishing Corp., New York, 1954.

Giedion, Sigfried, *A Decade of New Architecture,* Editions, Girsberger, Zurich, 1951.

Gropius, Walter, *Scope of Total Architecture,* Harper & Brothers, New York, 1955.

Hamlin, Talbot, *Architecture Through the Ages,* G. P. Putnam's Sons, New York, 1953.

Hamlin, Talbot, *Forms & Functions of 20th Century Architecture* (4 vols.), Columbia University Press, New York, 1952.

Hamlin, Talbot, *Architecture, an Art for All Men,* Columbia University Press, New York, 1947.

Hatje, Gerd; Hoffman, Hubert; and Kasper, Karl, *New German Architecture,* Praeger, New York, 1956.

Hitchcock, H. R., and Bauer, C. K., *Modern Architecture in England,* Museum of Modern Art, New York, 1937.

Hitchcock, Henry-Russell, *In the Nature of Materials,* Duell, Sloan and Pearce, New York, 1942.

Hitchcock, Henry-Russell, *J. J. P. Oud,* Editions, "Cahiers d'art," Paris, 1931.

Hitchcock, Henry-Russell, *Latin American Architecture Since 1945,* Museum of Modern Art, New York, 1955.

Hitchcock, Henry-Russell, *Modern Architecture, Romanticism and Reintegration,* Paysen & Clarke, Ltd., New York, 1929.

Hitchcock, Henry-Russell, and Drexler, Arthur (eds.), *Built in USA, Postwar Architecture.* Museum of Modern Art. Simon & Schuster, New York, 1952.

Hitchcock, Henry-Russell, and Johnson, Philip C., *The International Style,* W. W. Norton, New York, 1932.

Holmdahl, G., Lind, E., Odeen, K., *Gunnar Asplund Architect,* Svenska Arkitekters, Riksforbund, Stockholm, 1950.

Hood, Raymond M., *Raymond M. Hood,* McGraw-Hill, New York, 1931.

Johnson, Philip C., *Mies van der Rohe,* Museum of Modern Art, New York, 1947.

Koike, Shinji, *Contemporary Architecture of Japan,* Shokokusha, Tokyo, 1954.

Koike, Shinji, *Japan's New Architecture,* Shokokusha, Toyko, 1956.

Koyl, George S., *American Architects Directory,* American Institute of Architects, Bowker, New York, 1955.

Le Corbusier, *Le Corbusier et Pierre Jeanneret—Oeuvre Complète de 1929-1934,* W. Boesiger, Les Editions d'Architecture Erlenbach, Zurich, 1946.

Le Corbusier, *Le Corbusier et Pierre Jeanneret—Oeuvre Complète de 1934-1938,* Max Bill, Les Editions d'Architecture Erlenbach, Zurich, 1947.

Le Corbusier, *Le Corbusier—Oeuvre Complète 1938-1946.* W. Boesiger, Les Editions d'Architecture Erlenbach, Zurich, 1946.

Le Corbusier, *Le Corbusier—Oeuvre Complète, 1946-1952,* W. Boesiger, Zurich, 1955.

Le Corbusier, *Le Corbusier—Oeuvre Complète 1952-1957,* W. Boesiger, Zurich, 1957.

Le Corbusier, *Towards a New Architecture,* The Architectural Press, London, 1952.

Le Corbusier, *The modulor; a harmonious measure to the human scale universally applicable to architecture and mechanics,* Harvard University Press, Cambridge, 1954.

Le Corbusier, *When the cathedrals were white; a journey to the country of timid people,* Reynal, New York, 1947.

McCallum, Ian Robert, *A Pocket Guide to Modern Buildings in London,* The Architectural Press, London, 1951.

Mills, E. D., *The New Architecture of Great Britain,* The Standard Catalogues Co., Ltd., London, 1953.

Mindlin, Henrique, *Modern Architecture in Brazil,* Reinhold, New York, 1956.

Mock, E. (ed.), *Built in USA 1932-1944,* Museum of Modern Art, New York, 1944.

Mondrian, Piet, *Plastic Art and Pure Plastic Art, 1937 and Other Essays, 1941-1943,* Wittenborn, New York, 1945.

Morris, William, "The Revival of Handicraft," *Architecture, Industry and Wealth,* Longmans, Green, London, New York, 1902.

Mumford, Lewis, *From the Ground Up,* Harcourt, Brace, New York, 1956.

Museum of Modern Art, *What is Modern Architecture,* Simon and Schuster, New York, 1946.

Nelson, George, *Industrial Architecture of Albert Kahn,* Architectural Book Publishing Co., New York, 1939.

Neuenschwander, Eduart, *Finnische Bauten,* Verlag fur Architectur, Zurich, 1954.

Neutra, Richard, *Survival Through Design,* Oxford University Press, New York. 1954.

Pagani, Carlo, *Architettura Italiana Aggi,* Hoepli, Milan, 1955.

Papadaki, Stamo, *The Work of Oscar Niemeyer,* Reinhold, New York, 1950.

Pedersen, Johen, *Arkitekten Arne Jacobsen,* Arkitektens Forlag, Kobenhava, 1954.

Peter, John, and Weidlinger, Paul, *Aluminum in Modern Architecture,* Vols. I and II, Reynolds Metals Company, Louisville, Kentucky, 1956.

Pevsner, Nikolaus, *Pioneers of Modern Design,* Museum of Modern Art, Simon and Schuster, New York, 1949.

Pevsner, Nikolous, *Pioneers of Modern Design from William Morris to Walter Gropius,* Museum of Modern Art, New York, 1949.

Richards, J. M., *An Introduction to Modern Architecture,* Penguin Books, New York, 1947.

Roth, Alfred, *La Nouvelle Architecture,* H. Girsberger, Zurich, 1940.

Roth, Alfred (ed.), *The New Architecture,* Les Editions d'Architecture Erlenbach, Zurich, 1946.

Ruskin, John, *The Seven Lamps of Architecture,* Longmans, Green, New York, 1909.

Ruskin, John, *The Stones of Venice,* Lovell, New York, 1851.

Sartoris, Alberto, *Encyclopedie de l'Architecture Nouvelle,* Hoepli, Milan, 1954.

Smith, G. E. Kidder, and Everard, George, *Italy Builds,* Reinhold, New York, 1954.

Smith. G. E. Kidder, *Sweden Builds,* Reinhold, 1957.

Smith, G. E. Kidder, *Switzerland Builds,* Bonnier, 1950.

Sullivan, Louis H., *The Autobiography of an Idea,* Dover Publications, New York, 1956.

Sullivan, Louis H., *Kindergarten Chats and Other Writings,* George Wittenborn and Co., Inc., New York, 1947.

Whittick, Arnold, *European Architecture in the 20th Century,* Crosby Lockwood, London, 1950-1953.

Whittick, Arnold, *Eric Mendelsohn,* Leonard Hill Books, London, 1956.

Van de Velde, Henri, *Zum Neven Stili,* R. Piper, Munich, 1955.

Vitruvius, *On Architecture* (2 vols.), G. P. Putnam's Sons, 1931.

Viollet le Duc, *Lectures on Architecture,* Sampson, Low, Marston, Searle & Rivington, London, 1877-1881.

Wright, Frank Lloyd, *An Autobiography,* Duell, Sloan and Pearce, New York, 1943.

Wright, Frank Lloyd, *When democracy builds,* University of Chicago Press, Chicago, 1945.

Wright, Frank Lloyd, *Frank Lloyd Wright on Architecture, selected writings 1894-1940;* ed. with an introduction by Frederick Gutheim, Duell, Sloan and Pearce, New York, 1941.

Wright, Frank Lloyd, *The Story of the Tower,* Horizon Press, New York, 1956.

Wright, Frank Lloyd, *The Future of Architecture,* Horizon Press, New York, 1953.

Wright, Frank Lloyd, *Genius and the Mobocracy,* Duell, Sloan and Pearce, New York, 1949.

Wright, Frank Lloyd, *An American Architecture,* ed. Edgar Kaufmann, Horizon Press, 1955.

Wright, Frank Lloyd, *The Natural House,* Horizon Press, New York, 1954.

Wright, Frank Lloyd, *A Testament,* Horizon Press, New York, 1957.

Zevi, Bruno, *Storia dell'Architettura Moderna,* Giulio Einaudi, Turin, 1953.

Periodicals:
Architectural Forum, New York.
Architectural Record, New York.
Architectural Review, London.
L'Architecture d' Aujourd'hui, Paris.
L'Architettura. Rome.
Arts and Architecture, Los Angeles.
Bauhen-Wohen, Zurich.
Domus. Milan.
Habitat, São Paulo.
Progressive Architecture, New York.
Time, New York.
Werk, Zurich.

Skidmore, Owings & Merrill, 182–183, 190–191, 198–200, 213, 214, 215, 218, 222
Sullivan, Louis Henri, 16, 17, 20, 29, 222
Tange, Kenzo, 27, 178–179, 213, 222
Tecton Group, 153, 156, 210, 211, 222
Terragni, Giuseppe, 27, 150, 210, 222
Thompson, Benjamin (see Architects' Collaborative)
Torroja, Eduardo, 27, 102–103, 134–135, 205, 208, 222

Twitchell, Ralph S., 174, 212, 222
de Valesco, Juan Martinez (see Juan O'Gorman), 177, 213, 221
van der Vlugt, L. C., 138, 208, 217, 222
Vasconcelos, Hernani (see Ministry of Education), 106–107, 206
Villanueva, Carlos Raul, 27, 184–185, 214, 222
Vitellozzi, Annibale, 136, 168–169, 208, 212, 218, 221, 222
Wright, Frank Lloyd, 17, 21, 26, 41–61, 201, 202, 222
Yamasaki, Minoru, 27, 192–193, 214, 218, 219, 222

INDEX OF STRUCTURES

INDEX OF BUILDING TYPES